THE POWER OF THE
MIDDLE GROUND

MARTY BABITS, LCSW, BCD

THE POWER OF THE
MIDDLE GROUND

A Couple's Guide
to Renewing
Your Relationship

Prometheus Books

59 John Glenn Drive
Amherst, New York 14228–2119

Published 2009 by Prometheus Books

Inquiries should be addressed to
Prometheus Books
59 John Glenn Drive
Amherst, New York 14228–2119
VOICE: 716–691–0133, ext. 210
FAX: 716–691–0137
WWW.PROMETHEUSBOOKS.COM

13 12 11 10 09   5 4 3 2 1

Library of Congress Cataloging-in-Publication Data

Babits, Marty, 1948–
    The power of the middle ground : a couple's guide to renewing your relationship /
by Marty Babits.
        p. cm.
    ISBN 978–1–59102–662–4 (pbk.)
    1. Marriage counseling. 2. Communication in marriage. 3. Couples—
Psychology. I. Title.

HQ10.B32 2008
646.7'8—dc22

                                                                            2008030586

Printed in the United States of America on acid-free paper

To the memory of my parents,
Rose and Seth,
and my dear sister, Linda.

With love always.

CONTENTS

couples—most notably societal and internalized homophobia, which require special attention.

Evaluate whether you, in spite of having child-centered issues to attend to, are paying enough attention to nurturing your love relationship.

ground: (1) Meeting, (2) Pink Sun, (3) New Light,
(4) New Sound.

FOREWORD

Dr. Ronald Taffel,
Executive Director of the Institute
for Contemporary Psychotherapy

At this moment in time, in both practical and theoretical ways that affect our families, our personal lives, and our intimate relationships, Marty Babits steers us in a powerful direction that belies the usual associations with finding a "middle ground," as in the name of his exciting new book. The middle ground has nothing to do with compromising on what you want and need, nothing to do with dulling down your dreams and expectations. Instead, Babits has designed an approach that allows partners to connect to each other more vitally, without losing themselves in the process.

In this cyber-driven world, eyes are continuously trained to screens with rapidly shifting images; attention spans have grown famously short and jumpy. Responding to this cultural reality, Babits guides us in seeing differently—by taking advantage of the powerful middle-ground perspective. In discovering it, we learn to take stock of what we really need and want and what we can create with our partners. We are guided in developing a sustained vision that anticipates what to do in order to be and stay connected to ourselves and to each other. We are instructed on the means to develop the modicum of patience necessary to get the job done.

Why bother to find the middle ground that lies between you and your partner, you might ask? In a world gone mad with extreme thinking, the ability to find the middle ground, both concretely and metaphorically, is an antidote to the pressures that keep us from realizing, with our partners, what we hold most dear. For example, our children are subjected to all-or-nothing testing regimens that put their futures at risk in the early grades. Many of us mistakenly associate extreme positions with positions of strength. In the media, in politics, and in our personal lives, we are beset with an onslaught of extremes. Yet as anyone in a relationship knows, there are periods and moments in which stuck, dead interludes of noncommunication require ongoing and not extraordinary (or extreme) measures. Instead, attention to hot spots calls for steady, sustainable strategies such as are offered here.

While we, as a culture, look to Mars-Venus extremes for understanding, Babits talks about the middle ground in a new language that both men and women can understand, taking great care to point out ways that you can—as a result of sharply drawn and resonant unpacking of couples' problems—find yourself, in the anecdotes and vignettes he shares and in your own relationships as you learn about the concepts and try out the exercises.

But the very idea of change itself has become culturally radicalized, filled with illusions of immediate action and instantaneous results. In doing the work of finding the middle ground in your own relationship with your partner, you are brought into another realm—a keen awareness of what it means to grapple with the process of change itself. The discussion of difficulties inherent in the change process, especially in regard to positive change, marks an area in which this book makes a particularly fine contribution. Babits helps partners develop a kind of mental toughness that can help foster the emotional stamina necessary for relationship repair. Do not expect to find cookbook or impossible-to-believe makeovers here. This approach explores learning how to change in a down-to-earth manner, elucidating the process and the support required.

This aspect, which Babits spends a great deal of time walking the reader through, is essential to get into one's bones—change does not happen from one nanosecond to the next, and it most often involves increased capacity for frustration tolerance, which includes frustration with our partner as well as with ourselves. Underscoring the difficulties inherent in change is the understanding that opportunities for connection and growth are embedded, but remain underutilized, in many instances and aspects of our lives. The middle ground here involves neither overestimating nor underestimating the difficulties inherent in change. Using an accessible, optimistic approach, Babits helps couples develop opportunities for rebuilding love and passion.

In its intention, conception, exercises, and vivid case examples, this volume is not just another how-to but a way of thinking about and constructing what those of us in twenty-first-century relationships need to communicate effectively with one another, connect with one another, in order to change what needs to be changed. It has always been my experience that people do not fully respond to work like this unless the work has a combination of transcendence and magic as well as being absolutely practical and lucid. And that is what you'll experience here.

The middle ground becomes a concrete way of enlivening and perhaps saving relationships. It is a way of creating a home for our relationships. Lifelessness or living life on a precipice of anxiety and anger are conditions that many face regularly. The middle ground is an antidote to these conditions. The middle ground is where the heart of a relationship's aliveness, its resilience, is located. It is the part of the relationship in which couples, together, can develop the patience and accommodate the fierceness of their love and need for each other.

The middle ground is a potential that exists within love's province, in which the hard-edged realities of keeping a contemporary relationship vital can be found.

PREFACE

In my practice as an educator, a couples' therapist, and a supervisor of couples' therapists, I have cared for people undergoing relationship turmoil for more than twenty-five years. From this experience, I have developed a framework and a method for reestablishing emotional safety in a troubled partnership—and I now offer these to you.

The framework comprises a cluster of interconnected ideas I call the "middle ground"; these concepts empower partners to negotiate differences, emphasize the positive, see issues from each other's point of view, defuse anger, and, as a result, rekindle warmth and love.

The method consists of a series of exercises that bring the conceptual framework alive experientially for those who work with them. For instance, one exercise specifically prepares you to express feelings without ramping up anger, even though you may feel angry or critical or both. The middle ground is not simply an idea, but it is a way of approaching solutions to relationship problems, giving you an immediate edge. By stepping into the middle ground, you step away from patterns that reinforce the habitual and prolonged difficulties that have motivated your search for better ways of being with your partner.

I am going to teach you how to mine your relationship for its maximum healing potential. Although each couple has unique qualities, very many share similar problems. Some partners, strange as it may sound, begin their attempt at healing with the belief that their problems cannot be healed. Very often this is not based on a realistic appraisal of their problems but upon a despair that predates the relationship itself.

Please understand this—I do not champion mindless optimism. I want to develop mindful optimism. Here's the difference: Mindless optimism results from a rigidly held mind-set that bears little relation to the situation at hand; it is a mechanical attitude that gets automatically applied to any and all situations. Mindful optimism is a function of being alive and responsive to real possibilities for positive change. Mindless optimism is essentially passive; mindful optimism is active and engaged. Why is it so important to be mindful? Because you can't take advantage of opportunities for good change unless you are attuned to how and when the moments enter your awareness. Sometimes these opportunities come up like inexplicable gifts of providence, and sometimes they take the form of unfortunate circumstances that, nonetheless, give rise to breakthroughs in togetherness.

I will help you resist making judgments about what will best heal your relationship until after you've utilized the various ideas, techniques, and suggestions you'll find here. Although elemental, this is a key point.

In this volume, I offer targeted advice to heterosexual and gay couples, marrieds, and live-ins, couples with children, childless couples, and older couples. Throughout the book, you will find exercises, suggested activities, and checklists to take you beyond the blues.

ACKNOWLEDGMENTS

The keen insight and wisdom of my mentor and colleague, Dr. Allen Bergson, helped make the successful completion of this project possible. Dan Smullyan read many sections of the manuscript —some a number of times—and offered cogent responses that helped me develop and shape my ideas. I am extremely grateful to each.

Dr. Ron Taffel, Dr. Judith Friedman, Rosemary Masters, and Lois Nachamie read early versions of the manuscript and gave me valuable feedback and important encouragement. My affiliation with the Institute for Contemporary Psychotherapy in Manhattan, as home base for my clinical and professional growth, has enriched my work and life enormously.

The Family and Treatment Service executive supervisory committee—including Fran Hamburg, Jacqueline Schatz, Juliana Neiman, Janet David, Ella Lasky, Judi Price—I thank you for your support.

The KV crew, including Bob Nathanson, Allen Silverstein, Murray Schefflin, David Bellel, Richard Karney, Marvin Kuperstein —my punchball buddies—all offered support and encouragement throughout the writing process. Stewart Brokowsky, in memoriam, imparted courage.

My son Lucas offered key technological help; nephew, Matthew Devin; nieces, Nicole and Felicia; and my lovely sisters, Jane and Olivia, all provided support as needed.

Special thanks to Dr. Elizabeth Danto; Paula Eagle, MD; Dr. Suzanne Iazenza; and Hillary Mayers for timely and generous responses.

My crew at the Board of Education—Shifra Levin, Suzanne Carmona, Maria Ramirez, Patrick Walsh. I thank you from the bottom of my heart for your respective gifts of friendship, brotherhood, sisterhood.

I thank Nancy Rosenfeld, my agent, who guided me through the process of finding a publisher. Leslie Levine, thanks for your sage consultation. Julia Mosha, I appreciate your talent and professionalism, your editorial assistance helped me more than you know. I thank Heather Ammermuller, my editor; Chris Kramer; Jill Maxick; Mark Hall; Grace Zilsberger; and most especially Steven L. Mitchell for providing a home for me and the middle ground at Prometheus Books.

The couples I have worked with deserve a place of honor here. Without your trust and commitment to the middle-ground process, this book would never have been written. And to all others—friends, relatives, colleagues, supervisors, supervisees—whose names belong here but have not been mentioned, please forgive my omission; naming all would be impossible, but I wish to express appreciation for every ounce of the help and support I have gotten from many places and people and without which I could not have explored and developed my ideas. Thank you. I am indebted to you all.

INTRODUCTION

T he idea of the middle ground emerged from my efforts to make sense of my own difficulties in communicating with my partner.

Julie and I had argued—something we did a lot of in those days—raising our voices on an otherwise splendid autumn day. I had lost my temper and regretted some things I'd said and some that had occurred to me to say only after it was too late to ease our senseless argument. The moment passed, and my anger began to subside.

Our arguing often left us both feeling emotionally drained and defeated, and it did on that day. Perhaps I had merely forgotten to lower the seat on the toilet after using it. Often it was about such monumental issues. I'm not sure what it was I'd done, but whatever it was proved strong enough to provoke Julie into temporary amnesia concerning any and all positive characteristics she had previously credited me with.

Many years later, I have come to see that we were really fighting with ourselves in each other's presence, not fighting with each other. I realize now that the problem was that neither of us had evolved to the point where we felt secure enough within ourselves to risk giving up even one iota of personal prerogative, for fear that not only would that iota never be recovered but that it would precipitate an avalanche of chaos within each of our fragile self-systems. We feared that this chaos would leave us in a state of fear and trembling in which we would be unrecognizable even to ourselves—this is the dread of losing yourself in a relationship because the relationship demands that, as a prerequisite, you have already established a reliable (and shareable) identity within yourself. And neither of us, at that point, were on such terms with who we were. Needless to say, with two such tenuous egos in tandem, conversations were touchy.

When I had calmed down sufficiently, I suggested we go for a walk together. I was hoping to soothe our frayed nerves and undo whatever hurt we could.

We wandered up the avenue in the bright sunshine. Carpenters were constructing a stage nearby. A bright blue sign informed us of an outdoor jazz concert on 106th Street, also known as Duke Ellington Boulevard, later that afternoon. We talked about hearing live music together, something we hadn't done in quite a while but had previously enjoyed. A few blocks' stroll had me feeling miles from the useless argument.

We then turned up toward a bookstore on Broadway that displayed tables of books—most new and deeply discounted—under an attractive green awning in front of the store entrance. Although the shop was not too far from where we lived, I rarely passed it.

A year earlier, I had chanced upon a book on one of those display tables, reduced by eighty percent, that was enormously helpful to me, positively inspirational. A book about hope—a subject I had been thinking and writing about at the time—in a way that lifted a veil of mystification and allowed me to see my own thoughts clearly. That the book had cost next to nothing and had been so valuable to me had made its discovery feel like kismet.

As we approached the spot where I had found that volume, I wondered whether some other prize would fall my way. I turned to Julie and asked if she'd mind my glancing through the books outside the store. "It will only take a minute."

In my mind, the question was a pro forma courtesy. Why would she object to such a small request? How could she? As fate would have it—and my good fortune, in the end—she promptly replied, "I would mind. Let's keep walking."

Flabbergasted, I thought, *How could she be so self-centered? If the tables were turned, I would never do this to her. How does she expect me to feel, being with someone who would restrict me so unreasonably?* My face flushed. I remembered the heated argument that we'd had at home and my apology for losing my temper then. Yet, here on Broadway, my anger was spiking again.

I didn't want to lose control. I struggled to give myself a chance to think through what was happening. We turned into Riverside Park. In sharp contrast to my mood, the scene was tranquil. A mild breeze off the Hudson River wafted the scent of honeysuckle our way. Between the trees, I could see small boats on the horizon.

Julie seemed lost in her thoughts, and I tried to hold onto mine. If I released them in a gust I felt they'd carry one of those sailboats straight up to the distant George Washington Bridge. Another flurry of recriminating questions occurred to me as before but soon a new trend of responses formed.

How could she refuse such a small request? I thought.

First of all, the question struck me, was it a request? Can I call it a request if I get furious when she doesn't comply? Wasn't I demanding that she do what I asked? A demand isn't a request. Is that reasonable on my part? And in what sense was it a *small* request? I certainly was acting, at least within myself, as if this was *hugely* important.

I characterized her response as lacking in generosity, but if it was so important to me, why had I framed it so casually? Had I in any way communicated its importance? I didn't see where I had.

Even if she didn't think it was important to me, even if she believed it was casual, I asked myself, *Why would she want to deny me a little thing when it would be easy for her to be obliging?* This struck me as a key question, and it held my attention—applicable to so many situations that couples face. It would have been so easy for her to give me what I wanted, but she chose not to. Why?

I thought about the walk and, though the entire stroll may have been a small thing—by no means a major event in our lives—it symbolized our ability to make amends, to switch gears after arguing, and to share a pleasant moment. The meaning—the potential for healing—in simple acts such as this takes on importance.

I had suggested that, since we didn't spend enough time together, we should take a walk. She had agreed, expecting this activity to mean something in terms of us, but then I was suggesting that, sandwiched into the heart of our walk, there be time that I spend by myself, while she waited around for me. She may have felt that, in my asking her whether she minded if I stop to look at the book titles, I was unfolding invitation, not for her to extend herself for me, but for her to exercise her prerogative to do what *she* wanted. She took me at my word and voiced her preference: yes, she minded if we stopped. Was that so outrageous? Did I not explicitly give her the opportunity to say what she wanted?

On the face of it, I had requested, not demanded, that we stop, and she had responded in kind, in the terms that I had initiated.

I was indirect then resentful that she hadn't read between the lines and seen that I'd really, really wanted to stop. But if I'd wanted to stop that much, couldn't I have taken a walk over to the bookstore by myself? Why confuse it with this walk, this moment of potential healing?

Perhaps I was distancing myself from the intimacy of the moment. Perhaps my suggesting that she wait for me, in itself, was insensitive. Then for me to become furious when she voiced her preference for not waiting—although my fury had seemed so justified only moments earlier—my anger started to seem selfish and self-centered, certainly ungenerous.

For both partners in a relationship to feel nurtured and understood, a lot of turn-taking is necessary. My request may have been not as unreasonable as it was poorly timed, out of turn, and inappropriate in its immediate context. This doesn't mean that there can't be flexibility in the purpose of an activity, but the changeability of purpose can't be taken for granted. If either partner feels excluded from the decision-making process—from small decisions to major—the trend of mutuality is thwarted.

I had become very angry and self-righteous about Julie not wanting to stop with me at the bookstore. I, when I began to boil, couldn't imagine why she hadn't seen things from my point of view and compromised. But then I saw that I was invalidating *her* perspective with my reaction, or, perhaps more accurately worded, my reactivity. I had discounted, not included, her inner experience in my thinking—until I began to think things through. Much to my surprise, the more I thought about the situation, the more I realized that there was this other way of looking at things.

It wasn't a wild, mystical, invisible truth. It was a matter-of-fact ordinary other perspective. Other than my own, that is. It was commonsensical. But it involved a dialectic—an understanding of some relationship between my perspective and hers—both taken seriously.

CORE INSIGHT

I was amazed by the depth of my self-centeredness—that it could seal off any way of looking at the situation other than the one that occurred to me immediately. My perspective justified my feelings; therefore, I felt that my feelings were "right." And my perspective could be considered "right," but that still didn't make Julie's feelings or perspective "wrong."

This series of realizations freed me to think differently about what creating a shared perspective with Julie meant and what a shared perspective between couples generally is composed of. Plus, I understood the need to think about my own anger and modify the self-righteous confidence with which I tended to approach a conflict if I felt empowered—or perhaps the better word is "entitled"—by feeling that I was "in the right."

Where does the middle ground come from? From an *appreciation* of both partners' perspectives, understood separately and also together. A shared perspective. A perspective that encompasses two perspectives.

This experience became a living example, for me, of how intangible a middle-ground perspective can be, even if it is, upon reflection, central. Active reflection, akin to active listening, is the key to bringing the invisible into view, transforming the elusive into the obvious. Isolation into connection. Blame into understanding.

EXERCISE: MIDDLE-GROUND RESPONSES

Consider whether each statement is mostly or all true for you or mostly or all false.

1. When my partner offers an opinion or comment, I often interpret it as a criticism.
2. When I speak to my partner my intent is, except in rare instances, to be supportive.
3. It takes a lot for me to get angry at my partner.
4. We joke around a lot and rarely ever take things the wrong way.
5. It's hard for either of us to joke about anything without feeling the other will be offended.
6. When my partner tells me something about myself that I did not know or that I disagree with, in general, I take it to have some hostility in it.
7. Part of what I want and expect from my partner is for him or her to feel free to tell me something he or she may be aware of that I am not.
8. Generally speaking, if my partner is interested in something, I will tend to get interested in it also.
9. Generally speaking, when I am interested in something, my partner will follow suit and, at the least, demonstrate an initial curiosity—if not in the idea or subject then in my interest in it.

10. It's very difficult for my partner to surprise me; I'm always three steps ahead.

Scoring Procedure

Tally a point for each response that matches the answer key below.

1. F	6. F
2. T	7. T
3. T	8. T
4. T	9. T
5. F	10. F

Scores of 0 to 2 indicate a lot of anger and pain that needs to be taken seriously and worked on. *Scores of 3 to 7* indicate some middle-ground communication but significant pockets of difficulty require care and attention. *Scores of 8 or above* indicate a good amount of trust and comfort in your relationship. Most likely, with a score in this range, you have a fairly well-developed middle ground.

Chapter 1

WHAT'S THE MIDDLE GROUND?

M ost couples who seek help feel their difficulties center around communication. Carl and Amanda echo this concern when they consult me. At their first session, I ask, "What brings you to seek help at this time?"

"We don't communicate," Amanda replies.

"That's right," says Carl. "We have problems with communication."

I inquire, "But what brings you in to see me at this time? Why now?"

Amanda takes the lead. "Recently Carl lost his temper. That's been happening a lot lately but this time, the force of his anger frightened me. I said to myself, 'Something is wrong here.' I don't frighten easily. That's when I knew we needed help."

Not all couples complain of explosive anger as a key problem, but it is far from a rarity that I hear this complaint. At this point, Carl slouches back on the deep-purple couch and pulls a fringed pillow against his chest, as if it were a hot-water bottle.

Carl speaks haltingly. "She's right about what she said. There's something wrong, something missing."

"Can you tell me more about what is missing?" I reply. "Can you describe this thing that isn't in your relationship now? This thing that you need."

He nods his head, acknowledging my question; appears deep in thought; but, in the end, simply shrugs. My first hunch is that, like a lot of men, Carl grew up with little awareness that this skill—talking about feelings—would be so critical to his success or failure as a relational partner.

When Carl finally speaks, I learn that he feels like he is failing in his relationship with Amanda. He feels that, as a man, he *should* be able to maintain and project a stabilizing, reassuring presence. Amanda's growing insecurity confirms just how far short Carl has fallen. He realizes, without being able to stop himself, how hurtful his lashing out at Amanda is. He is unhappy about the relationship and about who he is in it.

Although painful for Carl, his dissatisfaction with himself is a potentially hopeful sign. Embedded within his dissatisfaction is the wish to make more of the relationship than what currently exists. Carl, unknowingly, is poised to discover that he *already* possesses sufficient motivation to make the positive changes that, as yet, he cannot visualize.

Couples who lack a middle ground, like Amanda and Carl, feel underappreciated and misunderstood. Each feels alone and lonely in the other's presence. Their attempts at communication end up in a power struggle. This situation is so common that it could be designated as the usual starting point for couples' work: *Square One.*

WHAT IS THE "MIDDLE GROUND"?

Imagine a place that brings the potential for love and compassion alive within your relationship. What would you call a place where you and your partner learn to communicate more productively? What would you call a place where understandings can develop from genuine differences? What name would you give a place in which natural capacities for sharing can be unfrozen and an atmosphere of emotional safety can flourish? I call this place the "middle ground."

If you are looking for help in your relationship, it's very likely you can't see this place clearly. Perhaps you've seen it but didn't recognize what you were witnessing. Perhaps you have never—not even within your imagination—had a glimpse of it. This is the middle ground.

This book will help you identify the middle-ground potential in your relationship and guide you in developing it.

GLIMPSES OF THE MIDDLE GROUND

Let's say your partner comes home in a bad mood and, rather than taking his mood personally—as an insult, a slight, a power maneuver—you wonder if something is bothering him. This puts you in a position to be an ally. Partners as allies—try to visualize this situation as it might pertain to you. Now consider what you see as a glimpse of the middle ground.

What does it take to support a middle-ground response like this, to be a good ally, a quality that many couples lack? The ability to weigh your responses, to fan out options, and to make choices rather than simply react as if on automatic pilot is crucial. And this requires a degree of patience, a rare commodity these days, but it can be developed. Every step toward the middle ground—including the exercises and activities found in this book—involves developing patience. Simply put, there is no way to sustain an adult partnership that does not require patience.

A second glimpse—Carol desires Kyle, but he is "not in the mood." Stung by his lack of understanding, his lack of generosity, she finds her patience is short. But instead of criticizing him, she decides to think about how to approach him so that they can have a conversation, not a screaming match.

Because she's given herself a moment of hesitation before blasting her partner, she can recall that it wasn't long ago that she had nixed his similar advances. She thinks, *How would I have felt if he had approached me angrily and complained about my not being in the mood then?* She realizes immediately that she would have been upset and angry; odds are, he would feel the same way if she approached him as if he were being ungenerous or lacking understanding.

This process—slowing down her reactivity and thinking about the situation rather than going with her knee-jerk response—represents a huge accomplishment, a step into the middle ground. Here, Carol gives herself an opportunity to *choose* what she does. Understand this as a gift Carol bestows on herself and her partner or, maybe even more to the point, an investment, one that pays huge dividends, particularly if the installments are deposited regularly.

In his fascinating 2005 book *The Paradox of Choice*, author Barry Schwartz cites research that demonstrates that negative emotion can have a detrimental impact on thinking and decision making. As studies show, when people are upset—under the influence of negative emotion—they tend to make poor decisions that do not represent their best interests. When we feel bad, it is almost as if someone else, a person who does not have our best interests at heart, becomes our proxy. Unfortunately, in a troubled relationship, we can be upset much or most of the time. That's not unusual. This means that while we sort out our relationship difficulties, we commit ourselves to a lot of poor decisions—which means a lot of misery—unless we can devise a technique for countering this trend. The middle ground is based on the understanding that people undergoing relational stress are generally *at their worst* and, for that reason, need to make their decisions with unusual deliberation. The material presented in these pages will help you modify your decision-making process sufficiently so that you can think about how you will proceed, based on the intended outcome you are seeking. You will learn to anchor yourself in this most important consideration. Do not go with your gut. Go with your reflection on what your gut tells you. Do not ignore your feelings, but don't let yourself be ruled by your feelings. Rather than function within the parameters of constantly judging who is right or wrong, most or least worthy, most or least blameworthy—instead of operating within those love-busting parameters, learn how to anchor yourself in the outcome you need for the relationship you want. Aim to extend your partner the benefit of the doubt, to invite him or her to respond to you when you express your feelings. Let your partner know you are interested in understanding their point of view as they understand it. That doesn't mean you accept, at face value, the way they see things. It means that you value their internal experience.

Carol thought about what she was going to do, about what she felt. What informed her thought process was, first and foremost, a process, not a discrete event. One thought led to another, and, somewhere in the chain of associations, she lit upon a very important middle-ground perspective—she thought about how her partner might react if she responded one way (with criticism and anger) as opposed to another way (with remembrance of how *she* felt when she was in a situation very much like his). Having arrived in the middle ground, Carol included a consideration of Kyle's feelings. As a result, what registers most strongly with him is that *Carol is an ally*. Their mutual bond grows richer through this sort of action.

This illustrates the sense in which middle ground relating creates a shared perspective. An incident like this can help your relationship a little; a pattern of these incidents can help your relationship a ton.

How can you develop a shared perspective if you do not learn to see your partner's point of view? You can't. But how can you learn to do this if it doesn't come naturally? This book answers that question.

WHY DO I CALL IT THE MIDDLE GROUND?

Locate the space *between* selfishness and selflessness. It results from cultivating what is possible, the inner edge of possibility. Discover the area between the way things are and the way they can be, this segment of possibility lies within the middle ground. Where mystification and despair are shed in the light of perseverance, creativity, humility, concern—this is the heart of the middle ground. *Middle ground* applies to the understanding that this area of the relationship belongs to neither partner. Neither can claim nor dominate this space; it is *between* partners, in the middle.

With tending, the middle ground grows sturdy and resilient; it can last a lifetime. Potential for intimacy, pleasure, dialogue comes alive here—though harm, even ruin, can come through neglect, cruelty, and shortsightedness.

DEALING WITH CONFLICT

Another glimpse of the middle ground.

Patricia and Annie argue about money frequently. Annie insists that Patricia is irresponsible with their money and lays blame for their problems—moderate debt—squarely on her partner. According to Patricia, Annie worries constantly and unnecessarily and cannot enjoy their life together. Patricia accuses Annie of being a killjoy; Annie complains that Patricia's spending is, if anything, increasing her anxiety levels and making it harder for herself.

Annie and Patricia have gotten into a destructive secondary pattern; they avoid making plans or spending time together, which reduces the frequency of their arguments but does nothing to solve their differences. They have become isolated from each other and fearful about the future of their relationship. By the time I meet with them, this pattern of avoidance has become more of a threat to their relationship than their original (financial) problems.

By working on communication exercises together, and through working at envisioning a lower anger level in the relationship, Patricia and Annie gradually tipped the communication balance away from avoidance and toward acknowledgment and understanding. Through their work, they recapture the element of tenderness that both had feared, during their angriest moments, would be unrecoverable.

With a modicum of goodwill and trust restored to the relationship, they were able to speak to each other about their respective financial concerns without becoming adversarial. As the work proceeded, Patricia gained new insight into Annie's anxieties about money. Where she had felt resentful that Annie treated her as a child, incapable of making responsible decisions about money, she came to see that Annie—because of a history of financial and emotional instability growing up with two alcoholic parents—felt helpless and childlike herself when faced with having to deal with even moderate debt. In other words, Patricia learned that being anxious about money was not something that Annie willfully inflicted on their life together but was an issue to which Annie was personally vulnerable toward. In fact, Patricia began to understand—once middle-ground connections were forged—that Annie needed Patricia's help in dealing with this issue. Patricia's ability to shift from a challenging to a nurturing stance helped lay the groundwork for a new and deeper level of trust and understanding to emerge between the two. They came to agreements about how to budget more collaboratively. In the end, money ceased to be a central obstacle in their lives together, and having been able to listen to and integrate each other's concerns about this very important issue strengthened their love.

Rage, impatience, self-righteousness will shut down the middle ground. Curiosity and a willingness to work on challenges (rather than avoid them) opens it up. The middle ground is not a measure of whether a couple has challenges to face—it's formed as a function of how couples react to the challenges they face.

AN IMPORTANT TASK FOR COUPLES: WHAT NEEDS WORK?

Middle-Ground Activity

Take an inventory of what's gone right and what's gone wrong. A balanced assessment will help you to zero in on what is most needed.

Allow yourself the freedom to identify and rank what you like most and what bothers you most about time spent together. Encourage your partner to join you in this activity. Comparing notes can be more than informative—it can help you take a first step into the middle ground. To assist you in preparing the inventory, I've provided a checklist to help you think through and identify problem areas, as well as a summary assessment form to help you organize your results.

Identifying Problem Areas

The most pressing problems in our relationship are:

____ The way we talk to each other.

____ We spend too little time together.

____ We spend too much time together.

____ We do not have enough relaxation time together.

____ We aren't romantic enough with each other.

____ We don't plan or cooperate around money well.

____ We do not make decisions together.

____ We socialize too frequently. We rarely have alone time together.

____ We socialize too infrequently. I feel we are an isolated couple.

____ My partner doesn't compliment me enough.

____ My partner is moody.

___ My partner stonewalls me.

___ I stonewall my partner.

___ I feel taken for granted.

___ My partner feels taken for granted.

___ My partner is too critical.

___ My partner talks down to me.

___ My partner says hurtful things to me.

___ I lose my temper too easily and/or too quickly.

___ My partner loses his or her temper too easily and/or too quickly.

___ My partner needs to know me better.

___ I need to know my partner better.

___ My partner's standards for neatness and/or cleanliness differ greatly from my own.

___ My partner does not stimulate me intellectually.

___ We haven't developed recreational activities that we enjoy together.

___ Our sexual appetites differ significantly.

___ We are not affectionate enough with each other.

___ Even when we are together, I often feel alone and lonely.

___ We can talk about problems, but nothing changes.

___ We do not celebrate the good things that happen in our lives.

___ We do not savor each other's accomplishments.

___ We don't talk about our feelings together enough.

___ We don't talk much about anything.

___ Our sexual relationship is less than satisfying.

___ We do not share equitably in household chores.

___ I do most of the social planning.

___ I am more outgoing than my partner.

___ My partner is more outgoing than I am.

___ My partner and I aren't good vacation companions.

For couples with children:

___ I feel like I do a disproportionate amount of work around the house.

___ My partner is a good parent, but I feel like my contributions are unappreciated.

___ My partner and I disagree about many child-rearing issues.

___ My partner and I disagree about religious issues related to our children's upbringing.

___ My partner doesn't do his or her share with the children.

___ My partner is controlling around the children and makes my help feel unnecessary.

___ My partner has a hard time collaborating in general.

___ My partner says hurtful things to me around the kids.

___ I say hurtful things to my partner around the kids.

___ My partner is too rough with the kids.

___ I am too rough with the kids.

___ As parents, we are a much stronger couple than we are when the kids aren't involved.

___ As parents, we are a much less well-coordinated couple than we are in areas where the children aren't involved.

And now let's think about strengths in the relationship (check all that apply):

___ We are considerate of each other's feelings.

___ We have common interests.

___ We have common values.

___ We are committed to each other.

___ We have activities we enjoy together.

___ Overall, sex is satisfying.

___ The level of affection in our relationship feels good to me.

___ I feel loved.

___ I feel appreciated.

___ My partner feels loved.

___ My partner feels appreciated.

___ We savor each other's accomplishments.

___ We support each other emotionally.

___ We support each other's career (or job-related) goals.

___ We talk to each other about important issues.

___ We are able to resolve conflicts by talking things out.

___ Overall, we are compatible.

For couples with children:

___ We handle chores related to the kid(s) equitably.

___ We respect each other as parents.

___ As a parenting team, we work well.

___ We are on the same page in terms of family-planning issues.

Summarize Your Results

Fill in the blank lines below.

1. The three areas that need the most work in my relationship with my partner are:

_____

_____

_____

_____

2. The three areas in my relationship I feel best about are:

_____

_____

_____

_____

EXERCISE: DO YOU HAVE A MIDDLE GROUND?

Rate your attitude to the following on a scale of 1 to 5, where 5 means you agree strongly and 1 means you strongly disagree. You and your partner should write your answers on separate sheets of paper. Then, follow the instructions under "Scoring Procedure" to see where you fall.

1. Before I speak with my partner, I think about whether it is a good time to deal with the issue I want to bring up.
2. Couples need to resolve stressful topics efficiently. Coming back to the same topic repeatedly indicates a poor relationship.
3. We have a number of shared interests and activities.
4. If I need to speak with my partner about something important,

I will push her to talk even if she protests, "This isn't a good time for me to talk about this."

5. When we disagree, a productive discussion will often help us clarify or resolve our differences.

6. Discontinuing conversation before an issue is resolved is equivalent to abandoning the issue.

7. Most of the time, my partner understands what I'm trying to get across.

8. If two people love each other, they should be able to agree on most important issues.

9. My partner listens carefully to what I say.

10. Agreeing to disagree is a sign of failure in the communication process.

11. When it comes to thinking through situations, my partner's style is very different from mine. Still, we manage to get beyond style and appreciate that we have a lot in common.

12. When all is said and done, couples should be able to work out problems without having to "work" at it too hard.

13. It's natural for differences to emerge in a long-term relationship. People are complex, and when you get to know somebody well, some of what you had thought was clear may become less so.

14. In my relationship with my partner, there are no surprises. We know each other too well for that.

15. Relationships provide a way to learn about aspects of ourselves that, otherwise, would likely remain beyond our awareness.

16. My partner's style is no more or less than a direct reaction to my style. If I say, "Black," he insists, "White."

Scoring Procedure

1. Total the number of points for even-numbered questions and for odd-numbered questions separately.

2. Subtract the largest score total from the other score total. For example, if odd-numbered questions total 20, and the even-numbered questions total is 10, subtract the even total (10) from the odd total (20). The score you have then is 10, with odd-greater. If even questions totaled 36, and odd questions totaled 18, the result would be 18 even-greater.

Charting Results

For odd-greater scores: 0–9 indicates that your relationship has some strengths but is in need of healing. 10–18 indicates possibilities for creating a middle ground exist but need to be nurtured with deliberation. 18 or above indicates that a middle ground exists between you and your partner.

For even-greater scores: 0–9 indicates very little goodwill seems to be established between you and your partner. It will take work to develop a foundation for the middle ground, but you may be closer than you think. There are some relationship strengths. If the score is between 10 and 18, a middle ground is possible, but trust appears to be in short supply. If the score is 18 or above, establishing a middle ground will challenge the ongoing trends in the relationship. Relationships in this area tend to be painful, and partners often feel despair about being able to regain a sense of hope and connection. With commitment, dialogue, patience, humility, and, for many couples in this range, the help of a qualified counselor, possibilities for middle ground can develop. This can lead to a new beginning in the relationship or, where appropriate, to a disentangling of hostilities, which will allow both partners to clarify their thinking and examine their goals and options carefully and constructively in an emotionally safe environment.

Chapter 2
RENAISSANCE IN LOVEMAKING

ROY AND MIRA

Roy and Mira began work with me feeling unappreciated by each other and lonely together—the "Square One Syndrome" I described in chapter 1. Their sex life had fizzled down to nothing. Each expressed pessimism about my help. Still, they were willing to try, which is good enough for getting started. Earlier in their relationship, they had felt good about their lovemaking and had been excited about their life together. They had lived together for two years and had agreed they'd marry somewhere down the line and have children together. Now in their late twenties, they felt dubious about ever carrying out those plans.

Early in our first session, Roy told me: "Mira retaliates for her unhappiness with certain things I do by withholding sex. I don't understand how things got to this point."

Mira responded, "In order to make love with Roy, I need to feel something coming from him that I don't feel. I feel discounted and disconnected."

Responding to a request from Mira to "make some changes," Roy said that he was willing to be different as long as he didn't have to be so different that he could no longer be himself. According to Roy, "I thought that when we started out, you loved me the way I was. I don't understand what happened. I haven't changed. Why can't you want me the way I am now? Why has our relationship changed?"

Aware of feeling deprived and uncomfortable, Roy showed little acceptance or comprehension of Mira's complaints. She tried to articulate it more clearly.

After listening to her describe what she felt, I volunteered to act as mediator and interpret what she had said for Roy: "She acknowledges that you do 'get' that she is unhappy, but she feels you don't connect that understanding to her needing something for herself, in order to feel good about herself and the relationship. Mira feels as if you are thinking or feeling that she acts the way she does in order to control you or get back at you. What she is saying is that primarily she is interested in feeling better and is unhappy and that, as a result of how she feels, she admits that she may do things that make you feel controlled or deprived—like not having sex—but it's *primarily* an expression of her wanting to feel better and express how she actually does feel. *Secondarily* it shows anger directed at you. But if you understand it solely as anger and not as coming from her wish to feel better, you are not 'getting' it."

I asked Mira whether I'd captured what she was saying, and she agreed. I questioned Roy if he understood what she was trying to say.

"I think so, but I also feel confused," he replied.

Roy's failure to acknowledge the reality of Mira's feelings of dissatisfaction within herself—and not simply as a weapon she was using against him—left her feeling invisible, empty, disappointed, and enraged. Rather than cherishing and nourishing her, she believed he experienced her feelings as a burden. This led her to question his love, which made him eminently unattractive to her as a sexual partner.

Mira recalled Roy approaching her, during the previous weekend, with a kiss and an offer of a glass of wine. This was, according to Mira, his way of signaling that he wanted to make love. "Otherwise, there're no kisses and no gracious offerings of wine," she reported. She'd accepted the wine but made clear to him that she was not in the mood. When he'd asked why she'd felt this way, she explained, "I'm feeling far away from you. We haven't talked to each other all day."

Roy had retorted, "Well, why don't we talk now?"

Mira had replied, "You just don't get it. You don't understand what I need. I've got to feel connected before we get to this point where you are trying to hold me and kiss me. That's what I need."

In my office, Roy reaffirmed, "She's right. I don't get it."

I asked if there was anything else going on that particular weekend that was memorable. Mira recalled another talk they had had that same day. She recited the conversation, giving emotion to both of their words.

"I noticed that you didn't have a chance to get around to repainting the bathroom last weekend."

"You know I was preoccupied all weekend with the car. I didn't expect to have to deal with that at all," Roy had gruffly replied.

"I understand. I'm just reminding you because you had said that you would do it the weekend before, and I'm looking forward to having it done."

"I know you are," Roy had spat. "I didn't forget about it. It was just impossible. I'm going to get to it when I can. You don't have to remind me."

Mira reported that conversations like this one were common. "After feeling that he takes me for granted, I have no interest in making him feel good. Roy is right about one thing. The reason I am not interested in sex these days has to do with a lot of things that have nothing to do with sex."

> **Note:** At this point, there is no middle ground, no shared perspective. If I can help one or the other make a breakthrough into seeing the situation from the other's point of view, the opportunities for them to help each other work through these problems will become apparent. And this is what unfolded once they made middle-ground contact.

Mira's Perspective

Mira had given Roy a gentle reminder about repainting the bathroom, which he had committed himself to doing. The task was overdue; he had said it would be done the previous weekend, and without a reminder he had not gotten the job done. When he responded to her first reminder as if she were nagging him—with a harsh and impatient tone—she felt scorned. She confided that she'd had these thoughts: "Not only do I have to remind him because he ignores tasks unless he's reminded, but then he gives me a hard time about it. He should be thanking me for reminding him. As far as I'm concerned, tonight—and any night in the near future, for that matter—he can go fuck himself."

Roy's Comeback

On the subject of chores, Roy conceded that he hadn't done his part. This is how he expressed his view: "So I don't paint the bathroom. Does that mean we don't have sex? My appeal is limited to whether or not I repaint a bathroom? Does that make sense? If we quarrel about something, we still sit down and eat dinner. We don't say, 'Let's post-pone eating until we can work out this disagreement,' do we? Sex is an essential need, isn't it? Sending someone to bed without dinner is cruel, me and Mira agree on that. Sending someone away without sex, consistently, is cruel also. It's hurtful and blows the other problems way out of proportion. Mira's right, I don't get it. It doesn't make sense to me."

Where Do We Go from Here?

Roy spoke of a connection between nonsexual issues—like chores getting done—and the couple's sex life. He still couldn't muster clarity of Mira's experience of the situation. Given feedback and encouragement, Roy acknowledged that he did not understand what it meant for Mira to feel connected *before* the issue of sex was broached, *because* he did not think along these lines himself. However, he did acknowledge that there was an impasse in their communication process. Rather than, as he had done previously, place blame for their problems squarely on Mira for withholding sex, his understanding had begun to shift toward placing the responsibility for their problems on what is happening between them—which included what he was doing! This is an important change, which I welcomed and validated. The logic of Mira's feelings still eluded him because he simply didn't think about whether he, or anyone for that matter, felt connected; it wasn't just an isolated thought that Roy didn't grasp but a way of thinking that, at that time, he couldn't imagine.

Deborah Tannen writes persuasively about differences in the way men and women think about verbal communication. According to Tannen, women characteristically use language to create a sense of connection, while men use it to establish hierarchical structure between themselves and others. Roy had no appreciation for the importance Mira attached to connecting through conversation.

Repairing Damage

Roy recognized that Mira's feelings had been hurt by his response to her reminder about the chores. "I'm sorry that I hurt you. I didn't mean to. My response had nothing to do with you. I was just annoyed that there is so much to do, and I have so little time to do it in. I get irritable because of that."

What to make of Roy's response?

Let's consider Roy's response in two different ways. *If*—that's the proverbial "big if"—his apology represents a breakthrough for him, then it can help repair the damage. He would then be expected to follow up with sensitivity if Mira should remind him about chores in the future. This could soothe Mira's hurt, make her feel better understood, and move the couple in a healing direction. That's one way of receiving Roy's apology. A second way—and this was actually the way Mira talked about it in the session we had—was that he was giving lip service to feeling sorry because he had been "caught in the act" of being unloving to her. She understood his attempt at apology as an insincere attempt to deflect responsibility. She was convinced that, by claiming he was unaware that his anger about doing the chores was being dumped on her, he was rationalizing and still not coming to emotional terms with what was going on between them.

Mira countered, "I would accept his apology if it was offered for an isolated incident, but this is a pattern. Rather than kick himself for not planning well enough or for forgetting what he needed to get done, he kicks me for noticing there's a problem. I resent it. Then, when he wants to make love later in the evening and he's baffled about why I'm not in the mood, I feel all the more invisible. And angrier. The issue isn't whether the chores are so important or central to our lives. I want to know if, when we speak to each other, Roy is prepared to be considerate of my feelings! That's more important than the chores. Although I do need to feel he is accountable to his word and to what he commits himself to doing, I can make adjustments if necessary, but it's his responsibility to let me know if he's going to reschedule the painting to another day, not mine to chase after him. My position—when I remind him—is thankless, and his reaction adds insult to injury."

I validated the importance of Mira respecting herself enough to insist on having her feelings taken seriously by Roy. Roy seemed to have felt, at this point, that she clung to her position out of stubbornness, but I—and I made this clear to them both—felt that what she so resolutely clung to was the hope that they could heal their emotional connection. She held out for him to join her in a connection based on acceptance and appreciation of what they both felt within themselves; she was holding out for a middle-ground connection. To give up on this position would, in effect, be giving up on the relationship. Her refusal to give in to despair and anger was an act of relational heroism.

Hearing me describe Mira's position this way, Roy rested his chin in the palm of his right hand and eyed the floor momentarily. He then glanced up and acknowledged that he had pushed Mira away and that the chores had been an ongoing issue. "You're right. I should have apologized to you for needing a reminder and not acted the way I did. I see your point."

Something about his taking responsibility for the incident in this way appeared to reassure Mira. Still, she expressed wariness about whether he would follow through next time.

I said to Roy, "It's almost as if, for the first time, you see that Mira isn't simply trying to give you a hard time. You seem to be saying that you get the fact that you have been causing a lot of pain in her life. And you see that she is insisting that you understand what she is saying to you because she wants the relationship to work out but can't take it anymore if this is all there is going to be for her."

Roy stared at me directly. I could see moisture well up in his eyes. He turned to Mira. "I'm sorry. I do not want to lose you."

Mira teared up as he slid over to sit right next to her. He reached out and hugged her.

For so long, Roy had been holding Mira at arm's length, interpreting her unhappiness as a criticism of who he was—as if her complaints had more to do with attempting to make him feel bad than with making herself feel better, making the relationship better for both of them. Now he had internalized her words and feelings, finally allowing her message to move him. *Her feelings were included within his response.* She had reached him. He was not acting as if they were alone within each other's presence; he was acting instead from within the relationship. *He had entered the middle ground and found her there.* She sensed a new element in his presence and returned his loving embrace.

After a moment, Mira acknowledged feeling surprised at what she described as "Roy's much-more-open-than-usual response." Her praise for the openness of his response is important: *it is a partner's response to her partner's response that creates the middle ground.* A response that contains an acknowledgment of the other's contribution and feelings within it establishes mutuality. Such a moment becomes identifiable as a bona fide piece of middle ground. The possibility of these moments is ever present but, as we have seen, must sometimes be developed carefully.

> **Tip:** A response on your part that contains acceptance and acknowledgement—not necessarily agreement—of your partner's contribution and feelings creates mutuality in the dialogue. As mutuality is achieved, middle ground is generated.

Roy and Mira's Lovemaking

As you know, Roy and Mira's sex life had been faltering when they started to work with me. As anger had grown, their intimacy had dropped off proportionately. When their disagreements escalated into bitter arguments, both partners felt increasingly alienated and, eventually, despairing. Through ongoing therapy, the anger level gradually lessened.

Great communication does not guarantee great sex, but communication problems very often provoke sexual difficulties. Without having given the sex very much direct attention in our work together, other than asking about it occasionally, their sex life improved markedly.

These partners came in complaining about sexual dissatisfaction and an overall lack of intimacy. The last time I saw them, they were arm in arm walking out of my office, feeling good about themselves as a couple. Learning about the middle ground and how to achieve mutuality in their communication surely helped them. Other issues— anger management, dealing with unresolved family issues that each identified and worked with—also figured into their breakthroughs. By and large, they learned to work as allies, give each other the benefit of the doubt, and identify for themselves what their own style of working together felt like. Once they could do these things, they had transplanted their relationship from Square One to the middle ground, from despair to hope and love.

In this chapter, you will find two exercises, the Basic Three-Step and the Second Camera, that were extremely helpful to Roy and Mira in preparing the ground for their breakthroughs in communication.

Objectives

> **Key Point:** Having an objective undercuts a feeling of help-lessness, which undercuts feelings of anger and opens possibilities for clear thinking and effective action.

Mira complained that she and Roy did not talk to each other enough. Roy agreed that he needed to work on this area. In my work with Roy, he learned to initiate friendly conversation and then follow up with a focus on listening to Mira's responses. "The objective," I said to him, "is for you to express yourself *and* help Mira feel heard."

By helping him systematically review his immediate objectives in communication with Mira—as much as helping him grasp the specific objective under discussion—I impressed upon him the idea that by approaching his partner with clear objectives, he increased chances of making the positive changes he wanted. He confessed that, up until this time, he had not given much thought to how relationships, communication in particular, worked. He voiced a realization that working on relationships was important. I heartily agreed.

When I asked him if he was affectionate with Mira in nonsexual situations, he was a little uncomfortable. He told me that neither of his parents were affectionate with him. Roy agreed, during an individual session I conducted with him, that taking initiative to show affection for Mira in nonsexual situations would be a good goal for him. I coached him to do so. I also coached him to show receptiveness to Mira's nonsexual affection. His ability to make these changes, he reported to me, had been greatly enhanced by the fact that he had consciously targeted these objectives.

In the next couples session, while reviewing our work together, the topic of whether they were affectionate with each other in nonsexual situations came up. Mira told us that she had long experienced Roy's lack of affection as hurtful. At this time, they were sitting quite close to one another, and Roy took her hand in his and smiled sheepishly. "I'm working on it," he said.

She replied, "I know you are."

Touchstones

I suggested to Roy, "When you're in conversation with Mira, ask yourself this: 'What do I need to get out of this for myself and for our relationship?' That's the *touchstone* you need to keep coming back to."

Again, Roy looked confused, like he was trying to figure out if he had room for this touchstone in their tiny apartment, or maybe he would have to rearrange the living room furniture so it would fit.

I added, "Come back to this idea when you have doubts as to whether you are on course. Use it as a compass: What do you need to get out of this situation for yourself and the relationship? Stay tuned to this idea. Come back to this thought regularly, and it will help you locate the middle ground if you've lost your bearing."

I worked equally with Mira on using touchstones to help her break the habit of expecting to be misunderstood and to alert her to ways in which her residual anger toward Roy sometimes might surface inappropriately, considering all the progress they had made. Anger had become a knee-jerk response for Mira, and she now had to think twice about when it was or wasn't coherent with what was happening between them. I suggested that before assuming that Roy was not taking her seriously, she should remember that he was trying to change and that he needed her support to do so. Statements she had made, like, "I thought we had gotten past this; we're still stuck where we used to be," may have *felt* accurate to her but were not fair to Roy or herself and demoralized him, since he was really trying and she knew that. We invented a touchstone for her together, which she said came in handy when she got irritated: "Real progress. Sometimes real gradual. But real. It's real." Part of the reason it may have worked is that it usually made her smile to go through it. This mantra helped calm her and differentiate minor disappointments in the present from chronic disappointments of the past.

Inviting Dialogue

Roy and Mira, when I first began seeing them, did not invite each other to much of anything, much less dialogue. In fact, they barely spoke *with* one another; they spoke *at* one another. Neither allowed the other any breathing room to process what was said. They tended to react quickly and angrily. Both felt alternately attacked or put on the defensive; the listening process was shut down. Their dialogue, in which neither voluntarily participated, left them feeling like they were captives of (or at times escapees from) the other's anger.

After I coached them regarding the benefits a pattern of invitation might have on their dialogue, Roy made this comment to Mira, "I've thought about what you said to me," referring to the need for more conversation in the relationship generally, "and I think I'm getting clearer on what you are talking about. Can we talk about it more?"

He invited her to talk further. It may sound simple and straightforward, but reopening the discussion this way, rather than with reproaches, criticisms, insults, or sarcasm, made a huge difference in the tone of their conversation and their relationship generally. Roy and Mira reported an overall increase in civility and a reduced anger level, resulting from inviting—rather than trapping—one another in conversation.

Roy's invitation to talk further, among other things, validated that he'd taken Mira's message seriously and tried to make sense of it within himself; it demonstrated that he was working with her, that they were working together. I saw it as another validation of the middle-ground process that was flourishing between them. His message included an implicit acknowledgment and acceptance of her perspective within himself. She, in turn, decided to accept his invitation to talk, and this brought the interaction into the middle ground. The middle ground, in this sense, *always* entails a give-and-take process. The middle ground cannot be attributed to one or the other partner's actions or responses alone.

An invitation to dialogue is a simple but potentially profound gesture. A pattern of invitations can open a spirit of mutuality and represent a new direction for a troubled relationship. This is why inviting further dialogue is such an integral aspect of the Basic Three-Step exercise, described later in this chapter.

I worked with Roy and Mira to help them assess each other's availability for talking about problems, counseling them to postpone conversations if one could not handle discussing things in the moment, but I stressed the importance of scheduling a follow-up time to talk so that issues that needed attention could be addressed.

Invitations validate the decision-making capacity of the person invited. When you are invited to participate in something, you are free to accept (or not). You can choose. These golden notes—choice, freedom, acceptance—sound a chord that trumpets *middle ground*. Those to whom invitations are not routinely tendered tend to fluctuate between feeling either excluded from or coarsely directed to their relational spots. A dearth of invitations undermines the promise of feeling fully included in the thoughts of one's partner. And—because personal response to an invitation represents an ordinary but important mode of self-expression—a paucity of invitations makes having-a-say in dialogue more difficult. This frequently results in partners feeling "left out," and/or misunderstood.

Establishing Middle-Ground Rituals

I counseled Roy and Mira to think about things they enjoyed doing together and to consider scheduling these activities as regularly as practical. Certain patterns of connection gain power with repetition. They become much-anticipated rituals, offering reliable warmth and solace—activities like sharing a meal at home, dining in a favorite restaurant or café, taking a break together at a certain time of the day or the week, walks through nature or some other enjoyable setting, welcoming touches (erotic or otherwise), listening to music together, or reading poetry or prose to one another. Anything that you and your partner enjoy together can become a middle-ground ritual if you preserve space for it in your schedules. Even a specific topic of discussion, if both partners feel heard and alive within the talk, can repeatedly afford enjoyment and bolster a sense of togetherness, as can a setting that both delight in visiting together.

EXERCISE: THE BASIC THREE-STEP

Making Difficult Conversation Possible

Healing depends on connection, connection on communication. I offer you a straightforward method for making conversation productive. Using this method, you can broach difficult subjects in a controlled manner. When you or your partner (or both) are angry, this technique helps you slow down and focus on connection rather than combat.

In this exercise, partners take turns playing reciprocal roles; one is speaker, while the other is listener, then they alternate. At any one time, each partner plays one and only one role:

1. The Speaker brings up the content and forms the message to be communicated.
2. The Listener's job is simply to receive the message and paraphrase it to establish that the message has been received.
3. The Speaker can then affirm that the message has, indeed, been sent and received.

If, for any reason, the Speaker feels the Listener has missed an essential aspect of the message, the Speaker repeats that part. The Listener's job is then to include the "missing" material in the new paraphrase.

Both partners must be mindful of their role and respectful of their partner's. Each must focus his or her communication so that the other can respond and keep this structured dialogue alive. The form underscores both partners' willingness to demonstrate patience. The form is expansive: each three-step movement is capped with an invitation to link what is being spoken about to what needs to be talked about next.

This exercise is a microcosm of middle-ground contact in the sense that the communication is safe, meaningful, controlled, and geared to further enhance other safe, meaningful communication. Good communication spirals in a positive direction.

When I was a teenager, I studied karate. All the students learned to perform a series of ritualized movements called *kata*, which involved no direct contact with any other student but readied us to utilize the more advanced techniques competently. It's useful to think of this exercise as a basic interpersonal *kata*. If done with care, it will teach you something useful about slowing down the communication process, careful listening, getting in touch with your feelings in a constructive manner, and inviting your partner to join you in building safety and inclusiveness into your communication pattern. I encourage you to read and think about it but also to practice it with your partner if possible.

Too often, when couples experience difficulties, conversation becomes an extension of a power struggle. When this happens, conversation frustrates, separates, and distances partners. This exercise provides an antidote to this trend.

Basic Three-Step Communication Formula

Overview: Basic Three-Step Communication has three parts:

1. You state what you feel.
2. You state when you feel it (the circumstances under which it usually occurs).
3. You invite your partner to respond and join you in talking about what is bothering you.

Step 1—a statement of what you (the Speaker) feel. But it needs to be a specific kind of statement. The Basic Three-Step formula promotes *self-focus*. For example, "I'm annoyed," rather than, "You are annoying me." Or "I feel angry," rather than, "You are the reason I feel angry." The importance of this self-focus will become increasingly clear. It is critical.

Step 2—a statement describing when this feeling arises. For example, "I feel angry when you respond to me by yelling." Or "I get annoyed when you leave the toilet seat up." Or "When you're driving and you make quick shifts from lane to lane, I get anxious." These examples combine steps 1 and 2; the order is not significant. [Steps 1 and 2 combined form what is sometimes called an "I-Statement."]

Maintaining self-focus gives the listener an opportunity to connect with what the speaker has said because the elements needed for understanding what the speaker is going through have been provided. So far, the speaker's affect (awareness of feeling) and the circumstance in which it arises have been communicated.

Step 3—the speaker invites a response. This can take many forms: "Do you think we can talk about this?" Or "I hope we can do something different here so that I can feel more comfortable." Or even "What do you think?" Or "I wonder if you are aware of how I feel about this?" These invite the listener to dialogue.

By adding a component that *invites* response from our partner, we explicitly encourage a nondefensive response. The basic three-step ideally serves this triple function—*it is expressive and informative and invites response*; this promotes middle-ground dialogue.

An example of the basic three-step: "When you're driving and you make quick shifts from lane to lane, I get anxious. Can we talk about it?"

What Is a "You-Statement"?

A you-statement focuses on a quality of the "other." For example, "I've told you I hate it when you yell. There must be something wrong with you." Or "Why do you leave the cap off the toothpaste? I've reminded you a million times about it, and nothing seems to penetrate. You're hopeless." Or "The way you drive this car drives me crazy. I have never been in a car with a worse driver." You-statements do not inform the listener about the speaker's experience; instead, they convey the speaker's evaluation of the listener. Most often, they ascribe blame for what the speaker is feeling on the person to whom they are directed.

You-statements promote defensiveness and escalate anger. Many couples who seek counseling use you-statements regularly. Rather than invite continued dialogue or new understandings, you-statements cut communication off and make reconnecting more difficult. This style of communication creates problems, deepens rifts, and compounds existing difficulties.

Contrasting the You-Statement with the Basic Three-Step

Take this you-statement: "You can't go out and buy whatever you feel like. That's irresponsible. You have to talk about it with me so we can coordinate the budget." The typical result? The listener feels berated and defensive in response.

Instead, try the Basic Three-Step: "It makes me feel uncomfortable when you make large purchases without discussing it with me at all because we're on a tight budget, and we need to coordinate what we buy. I would really appreciate it if we could do things differently. Can we sit down together and work out a plan?" The listener may feel defensive but is likely to also feel inclined to take in what has been said, to attempt to understand why and how the speaker feels.

Statements like, "Do you have to be that way?" "Can't you express yourself in a more intelligent manner?" "What's wrong with you?" "How many times do I have to repeat the same request before you hear it?"—the old-fashioned name for these you-statements is "reproach." Sometimes the reproach isn't in the literal content of the words but in the tone of voice or body language of the speaker. Some people can make a seemingly neutral statement like, "You're taking a piece of cake now," sound as ominous and accusative as a felony indictment.

Basic Three-Step communication is not ordinarily perceived as an attack. You-statements almost always are—because they almost always are.

How often do you use you-statements with your partner? Reserve a line in a small notebook for each day and keep track of every time you make you-statements by entering a check. Think about how different things might be if instead of using a you-statement you had used the Basic Three-Step.

Some partners object to using this technique because "it means you have to think too much." Some say, "I want to be able to just be myself without having to think about what I'm doing all the time. It's too much work." I sympathize with this feeling. Improving an important relationship is hard work, and learning new ways of talking to each other is a big part of it. Staying stuck in old patterns may feel more comfortable—in the short run—but, in the long run, the choice is a no-brainer. Trying new approaches breaks the paralysis that often develops when partners have problems. Trying—the act of trying to make changes in itself—can mobilize your creativity. By resolving to try and make things work better for yourself and your partner, you activate the part of yourself that can *search* for positive outcomes. Being in this frame of mind can make the difference between working things out with your partner and remaining stuck in old patterns.

Awareness of the differences between Basic Three-Step and you-statement communication helps you monitor *both* the form and content of your messages to your partner. The idea is not to "water down" your messages but to make them function in your own, your partner's, and your relationship's best interest.

A Handy Acronym (And Review)

Here's an easy way to remember the Basic Three-Step formula: It may be the most important single A-C-T you can perform in reversing a pattern of blame and tension in your dialogue.

A stands for the Affect that you wish to express to your partner.

C is for the Circumstance in which it typically comes up.

T stands for the inviting your partner to Talk it over with you.

When you use the Basic Three-Step formula, you A-C-T in your relationship's best interest.

John says to Jenny, "Whenever I speak to you about my family, it seems you try to change the topic, and that really bothers me. Do you think we can talk about what's going on there?" Instead of saying something critical about Jenny, John described how he felt and when he felt it, and he threw the ball to her side of the court.

She was tempted to become angry and answer defensively. Instead, she simply said, "I'm glad you told me that. I wasn't aware that I was doing that. I'll have to think about how I feel when you talk about your family." Jenny's response included her feelings, and she followed up his invitation to participate in the dialogue by sharing a genuine feeling. Had John approached her with a you-statement instead of with a Basic Three-Step statement, chances are the dialogue would have been a repeat of their typical accusation-counteraccusation routine, the talks that they had come into therapy to try and change.

> **Try this:** Create a three-line diagram for two problem situations you anticipate. Put a capital *A* in front of the first line, a capital *C* in front of the second, and a *T* in front of the third. Then fill in appropriate affect on the first line, the corresponding circumstance in the second and a way you might extend an invitation to your partner to talk about the situation with you. Also, think of two situations in the recent past when you spoke to (or regret you hadn't spoken to) your partner about your feelings and circumstance and extended an invitation to talk. Do this for the sake of giving yourself practice constructing your own Basic Three-Step statements. The Basic Three-Step serves as a dialogue opener, not a dialogue closer.

An Insult Substitute

If you feel so angry that you can think of only insulting remarks, then substitute a straightforward statement such as, "I can't think of anything civil to say to you. I'm unhappy about this"—whatever is going on—"and I want you to help me change it." This will work much better than a put-down.

Although it is not easy to think about what you want to say in the heat of anger, having an "insult substitute" at hand can help avoid destructive talk. Blaming or insulting conversations lead nowhere, except to a lower rung of possibilities for healing. When you sense you are going down such a road, pull over and find another way to go. An insult substitute can help you change direction and avoid an accident.

A caveat: like any technique for improving human communication, there are times when Basic Three-Step statements will be more effective than others. No one technique succeeds in all situations. Attempts to approach changing the way people work with their emotions must be applied with humility and goodwill. If this technique (or any other discussed in this book) is used mechanically, as opposed to soulfully, favorable results will be hard to come by. The intent—to reduce blame and invite dialogue—must be joined to the form of the Basic Three-Step statement.

Make Love, Not War

The Basic Three-Step is designed as a peace-making procedure. What comes naturally to many of us when in troubled relationships is a version of interpersonal warfare. Using this technique will represent a significant change for couples who have become addicted to arguing. It's important to give yourself time to develop the habit of inserting this way of talking into the way you converse with your partner. It will pay off by restoring (or creating for the first time) a sense of emotional safety in your exchanges. It may feel strange because it is different, but isn't that the point of making changes in your relationship? You're striving to interact differently from the ways that resulted in feeling disconnected.

Patience, in terms of how couples talk to each other, means slowing down the communication process so that the time between remarks and responses allows for reflection. This makes the goal of communicating together as allies more possible. Slowing down conversation with the Basic Three-Step technique creates the spaces necessary for you and your partner to think about what is going on.

Many partners have not given much thought to the *form* of their conversations, much less to the *structure*. So this communication technique may seem strange to many readers, but it is neither difficult nor complicated. Most couples can, using this method regularly, achieve tremendous gains in communication over a short time.

> **Try this:** After grasping the basic form of this exercise, practice it at least three times a week for two weeks. Make it a point to deliberately *use* the technique in your conversations with your partner.

> **Bright thought:** Some people find the idea of recharging their communication process baffling. For many discouraged partners, their relationship outlook bears an uncanny resemblance to AAA batteries: hopes for long lasting coexist uneasily with expectations of disposability; the charge either holds or doesn't. End of story. But learning to use the Basic Three-Step counters this trend.

The Blame Factor

Simply put, blame murders love, shrinks patience, and swells anger. The exercise I'm presenting here reduces the element of blame in the way partners talk to each other. Why is this helpful? Blame shuts down capacities for listening because partners become preoccupied with defending themselves or counterattacking. Blame destroys hope for nurturing emotional safety within a relationship. Basic Three-Step communications reduce incidents of blame.

Many of the couples I work with need what I've detailed in this chapter—an effective method for speaking their mind, getting heard, and extending their dialogue toward mutual understandings. Understanding the Three-Step formula and the concept of you-statements is critical to middle-ground communication.

EXERCISE: SECOND CAMERA

An Exercise in Two Parts

Tip: Making use of the "second camera" unleashes the power of the middle-ground perspective.

Note on Procedure: Reading this exercise as you participate may feel distracting to your focus on participating in the exercise itself. If so, I recommend that you narrate it into a tape recorder and play it back for yourself as you engage in the exercise experience.

Part 1

Before you begin, take a deep breath. Find a comfortable place to sit where you will not be disturbed. Close your eyes if you like. Allow yourself to relax. Take a minute to think of an incident that exemplifies an important problem in the relationship that you want to work on, one that encapsulates the basic communication issues you and your partner struggle with. Do not push yourself to think of this incident; only let it come without any effort. Let it emerge from within your thoughts and feelings. If nothing comes to mind, simply choose any example of a fight or argument that you recall clearly.

Notice how you feel, how your body feels. If you feel any tension, take a deep breath, and as you release the air from your lungs, simultaneously allow yourself, to the fullest extent you can, to let go of the tension. Now, seated comfortably. shift your attention to visualizing the memory that you want to work with today. Attempt to recall everything about the experience that you can. Recollect the sights, sounds, smells, anything about the situation or time that you can recapture. Is it warm, cool, cold, humid, dry, sunny, rainy on this day? Are you outside or inside? What other details, if any, can you bring into the moment? The goal is to reexperience the incident, to "see" it as if it were a piece of videotape that you can reroll. In the replay, pay special attention to what your partner does. Notice aspects of his (or her) behavior that you find frustrating or difficult. Picture the behavior in detail so that you will be able to jot down as complete a description of it as possible. When you feel ready, open your eyes and depict your partner's part in the incident in writing with as much detail as you can render.

Part 2

Close your eyes once again. Relax your body as completely as possible. Reenter your focus on the incident you wrote about. Take a moment and allow your senses to recapture the feelings, sights, and sounds elicited within the scene. Now imagine that as you were focused on your partner's responses and behavior in memory, at that same time, another camera was recording the scene from a different angle. This second camera focused on you, placed so as to zoom in and out, as need be, and pick up everything that you did to contribute to difficulties in communication. Visualize what this second camera reveals. If it does not come to you as an image, try to recall or imagine the sounds of voices or the bodily sensations that you associate with the experience. If a "second microphone" rather than second camera yields more vivid results, then make the adjustment. Think about how to describe the gist of what is recorded by that second camera (or microphone). Did your responses to your partner move the interaction as you had wanted it to? Did your responses escalate the problematic aspect of the communication? Did you find yourself adding fuel to the fire once things had become difficult? Do you feel you made things better or worse? Can you recall an action or a statement you made that was specifically intended to deescalate anger? Take a minute to write down thoughts and feelings in answer to these questions.

Imagine that the perspective revealed by the second camera is similar to your partner's vantage point. How do you think your partner understood your responses or actions? Do you think he or she could see what you were intending to convey? Relax into this imagining. Even being able to make a small degree of headway in imagining this second perspective can be extremely helpful in working with your own and your partner's role in conflict situations.

Open your eyes slowly and write down as much as you can recall of this second perspective. Make note of anything that surprised you in what you saw. With hindsight, is there anything you feel you would have done differently? Anything you'd try that might be helpful in the future? Think about this and record your thoughts. Do not edit as you write. Simply get the thoughts down on paper. Any reasons that may have prevented you from acting in this alternate, more helpful way can be noted as valuable information. Do not include reasons here that center on anything your partner said or did. The purpose of this exercise is to develop clearer self-focus. Make this a list of reasons that pertain to your own style of dealing with the kind of issues that arose.

Conclusion

Once you have completed this exercise, you will possess a valuable self-assessment of a "classic" or typical problem you face with your partner and an analysis of ways that you can make inroads on improving the problem.

Take a further step and imagine what you think your partner will write when asked to complete this exercise. If he or she participates, you will see this version of the quintessential problem in the relationship. Even if you disagree with each other's way of defining the problem, your descriptions can be used as a valuable starting point for strengthening communication for you both.

Chapter 3

WHERE CAN A GAY COUPLE FIND TRUE LOVE?

A NOTE ON THIS CHAPTER

I will discuss my work with a gay male couple and a host of related issues that were pertinent to this work. Many of the issues and challenges faced with Rob and Mark are similar to issues faced with heterosexual couples and lesbian couples as well. Some are particular to gay male couples.

ROB AND MARK

Rob and Mark are both in their late twenties. Mark's meticulously trimmed beard and moustache, jet-black crew cut, large brown eyes, and swarthy complexion create a sharp visual counterpoint to Rob's clean-shaven face, wavy blonde mane, almond-shaped blue-gray eyes, and fair skin. Both are thin, but Rob, at approximately 6' 1", stands taller by a half foot. Mark's outfit strikes me as both oddly nondescript—brown bomber jacket, creased dungarees, thick Garrison belt, black T-shirt, Timberland boots—yet as precisely assembled as a standard-order uniform. At first meeting, Mark's mouth turns down in silence, and he avoids my gaze. Rob smiles and makes eye contact; he comments on the color scheme of the office and the relative ease with which the couple had found their way to me. In contrast to first impressions, I soon experience Mark's lively wit and learn that Rob, so seemingly easy and breezy, is suffering from anxiety and depression.

After asking a few basic questions, I learn that the men have been together for the past four years and living together the last two. For both, their partnership counts as the longest love relationship either has experienced. When I ask about their relationship history, Mark introduces his "two-month or ten-time rule." The rule is simple—no relationship of his could last longer than two months or ten meetings, whichever came first. I asked him who had enforced the rule.

"It's an operational principle, absolutely self-regulating," he replied. "Once I get my running instructions, I just go on automatic pilot."

Other self-regulatory directives, he explained, included an inability to trust anyone who showed him affection and a loss of interest in sex if he felt that his dating partner was thinking of him as a possible long-term partner. When Mark was faced with rejection or disinterest, he experienced an obsessive fascination with seemingly unreachable or unavailable men. He spat out this information in staccato bursts but then slowed to a smoother rhythm.

"All this until I met Rob, of course. He's the exception to all the rules. At least he was, or I should say we were. Sometimes I think I'm trying to be more than I am with him. I don't know if what we had is something I can be part of. Maybe it's not for me. You can't trick fate." Mark's lips were slightly upturned at the corners, but his eyes had no glint of playfulness.

His two-month or ten-time rule can be understood as Mark's personal version of this widespread and untruthful stereotype: gay men cannot sustain long-term relationships. The hackneyed cliché rests on a constellation of mendacity: gay men are promiscuous and flighty and lack the emotional stamina to sustain commitment. Mark had internalized these toxic precepts. Many gay men, whether conscious of it or not, have "learned" similar life rules, no less stringent and self-depriving than the guidelines Mark, before meeting Rob, had lived by.

"That's right, I've been more than I thought I was able to be with Rob in some ways, but recently I feel like I'm in it on my own." Mark's voice tapered to silence as Rob and I took in Mark's expression of loneliness and pain. How was it that he felt so alone with Rob there with him?

I wondered out loud, "Mark, it sounds like you feel hurt and angry. Can either of you tell me more about what is going on now between you? What has brought you in to see me? Why now?"

"Mark wants to open the relationship," replied Rob. "He wants to continue living together but have other sexual partners. For some couples, I can see an open relationship making sense, but for me and Mark, I think it might destroy us." He paused. "We are having a hard time. Involving other people in our lives now would confuse things. We need to feel like more of a couple."

I turned to Mark. "Rob is voicing a hope that you two can become more of a couple. Is that what you want, too?"

"I'm not sure I know how to be more of a couple, but I guess that's why we're here. If you're asking me if I can do that, I'm not sure. Aside from what I'd need to do, my part in making it happen, I'm not sure I know what being more of a couple would mean for us."

SUCCEEDING AGAINST THE ODDS

How often will heterosexual individuals face some form of social humiliation as a result of their choice of partner, given ordinary conditions? Rarely. But *not* having had this experience at some point would be the rarity for a gay individual.

Heterosexual couples become acculturated to understanding that by forming into a couple, they are doing what is expected of them. Layers of societal approval flow in the direction of accepting and/or validating the fact that the typical heterosexual couple be recognized for what they appear to be: a couple. It is not something—speaking in social terms—that must be achieved through struggle. Our culture makes it easy for a heterosexual couple to feel there is a "place" for them *as a couple*. If a partner in a heterosexual couple were to state he felt his community was against him *because they were a couple*, he would likely be thought to be suffering from paranoia, out of touch with reality. For a gay couple to state the same feeling would, more than likely, be perceived as credible, not improbable, perhaps astute.

Gays experience a negative and denigrating flow of disparagement, disapproval, and stark denial of their standing and status as a couple in many public and private settings. Long-term successful relationships achieved by gay couples represent, in the great majority of cases, a heroic struggle against the odds. Up until 1973, homosexuality was still considered, according to the *Diagnostic and Statistical Manual of Mental Disorders*, to be a pathological condition, a disease! Instances of professional and social ostracism—solely due to sexual orientation and/or preference—persist. The FBI continues to compile statistics on anti-gay hate crimes. The tragic slaying of Matthew Shepard still casts its horrific shadow over every compassionate American. And Shepard's murder, singular as it was, gave attention and visibility to a form of violence and discrimination that has plagued a population of victims of hate—men and women targeted, humiliated, beaten, sometimes slain solely because they are gay.

Although social homophobia is pernicious and has been all but ubiquitous in our society, internalized homophobia is arguably even more toxic and as omnipresent. Many individuals, gay or not, battle personal demons to achieve finally, if their efforts are successful, a sense that who they are is all right, that their self-acceptance is justified. How much harder does it make a person's battle for self-acceptance if *before* she can move toward it, she must *unlearn* messages—deeply ingrained and often unconscious—beseeching her to embrace the conviction that she is *unworthy of self-acceptance if she is gay*? That self-acceptance, given the influence of homophobic elements in our culture, is more difficult for gays than for nongays is indisputable.

In working with gay clients, a therapist, gay or straight, must be informed and knowledgeable about the extraordinary pressures and the trauma to which gay individuals—and couples—are regularly subjected. Some techniques used in dealing with the aftermath of trauma involve guided visualization. I fashioned a number of such exercises—available in full in Appendix 2—to use with Mark and Rob. Visualization techniques often make it possible for individuals to access deep and painful issues while maintaining a sense of emotional safety. This proved to be our experience with these exercises.

LEARN TO SEE WHAT IS NOT THERE

In order to create a portal of hopefulness for Mark and Rob, I wanted to help them see, within themselves, how things could improve between them. Currently their expectations, based on the fact that their sense of connection had been diminishing—brought them downward to despair. Wouldn't it be helpful if, rather than envisioning negative outcomes, they could access, as realistically as possible, what it might be like if things went well between them? My exercises involved using guided visualization to give them a chance to do just that—to see what was not yet there in their relationship but what might develop. With richly developed personal fantasies about how things might improve, I reasoned, they could steady themselves, get their bearings, differentiate between positive and negative expectations. But this would make sense only if I could help them generate a set of *positive* expectations. If they could do this, they would be able to see the difference between thoughts that were hope and love based and those that were despair and fear based. No longer blindsided by despair, they could gain more conscious control of their hopes and nurture them together. By opening this dialectic, my goal was to stimulate their emotional investment in the possibility of experiencing more positive outcomes in their relationship or, put another way, to resensitize them to possibilities for hope.

GUIDED VISUALIZATION

In the first visualization exercise, I narrated a story that depicted a couple, two men, who loved each other but were having relationship difficulties. (This guided-visualization exercise, summarized here, can be found in full in Appendix 2.) I intoned to Mark and Rob, "You see a couple, two men, who love each other. They look at each other, and there is so much about each other that they know. And there is so much about each other that they do not know. So much that they can learn about each other." I described the relationship as being in jeopardy. Despite loving each other, they argue frequently, and some arguments get overheated. Each feels bad about the way the relationship has been going. You can see the men are walking on the beach at dusk. They stand by the sea and gaze at the pink sunset. Far off at the side of the water, they can see traces of pink flicker against the outline of the moon. For a moment the sky possesses a crescent of moon and a sliver of sun. The couple walks along the beach together, slowly down the coastline. The waves splash lightly on the beachhead. Although there are worries, each feels the moment is calming and peaceful.

The scene changes, and we now see the two men sitting in a room. The season is no longer summer. They are comfortable together in their room. It is apparent—I narrate to Mark and Rob—that the two men have overcome a major hurdle in their relationship. They sit together feeling safe and calm. They have issues to deal with in their lives—both men do—but a wall between them has been cleared. The story ends here.

I asked Mark and Rob questions to help them imagine themselves in this couple's place, to help them "see" into their situation. For example, when I described the men (in the story) sitting together after having been on the beach, I asked Mark and Rob such questions as: "Do you see the men sitting close to each other? Are they holding hands? Are they talking together? Looking into each other's eyes? Are they laughing together? Are they hugging? What are they thinking?"

In the discussion that followed the exercise, Rob volunteered that he felt the men had come to a point where they simply couldn't stand repeating the same old fighting, the same old arguing. "They hit their rock bottom," he said. "There on the beach, they realized that things could be so much lovelier. They realized that they were missing out on what was important. And I'm thinking one of them, or maybe both at the same time, resolved to get a grip on their anger."

I replied, "Rock bottom? So it's like you see them having become addicted to their anger, their arguing. And the combination of feeling good on the beach and bad about things in general transformed one or both of them." I asked Mark what he thought about that.

"It's hard to fight against the sun and the moon. I think they just felt overmatched. I mean, if you can't read a message that cosmic, do you deserve love? Seriously." Mark had a wonderful sense of humor. He entertained with it, but sometimes, as in this situation, he seemed to use it to avoid feeling anxious or vulnerable.

There was a brief silence. Mark continued, "I like what Rob said. The thing that struck me about the story was that both of the guys seemed to find that turning point together."

"Maybe so," I said. "Do you think that's possible for people to do?"

"It's not impossible," Mark squinted slightly and gazed upward.

We spent time discussing the conversations the two men on the beach may have had that allowed them to discover solutions to help themselves. What was it that made the critical difference between them seeing their relationship as being in jeopardy at one point and then as feeling so much safer and calmer? What might have helped them across their impasse?

Rob chimed in. "I would say that they realized that they just had to do whatever it takes to put a lid on the anger. That they had to figure out a way to be better with each other. That they realized that they could have something together if they acted and if they let the moment pass, they'd have to separate. And I can identify with that because I feel like we've hit rock bottom, and that's why we're here. We haven't seen our pink sunset, but I am here because I want to try and work things out with you. I care about you very much. I'm sure about that."

Mark's gaze lowered, and he looked directly at Rob. "I care about you, too. I don't want us to end either."

I said, "You are both saying you want to see if you can make your relationship work. You both are voicing a wish to see the relationship continue on into the future."

Rob suggested postponing opening up the relationship. "I think we should give ourselves a chance to see if we can walk on the beach a little before we think about inviting others to join us. I want to end up walking with you, Mark. Not somebody else."

I asked Mark what he thought about holding off on outside relationships until we had a chance to get a more solid feel for how our work together would develop. After further discussion, both men agreed to a six-month hiatus on discussing or acting on the idea of opening the relationship.

WHAT COLOR IS YOUR MOOD?

Another guided-visualization exercise that proved helpful for Mark and Rob is titled "The New Light, Guided Visualization #3." The men were asked to picture themselves in a room, having a conflict or an argument. After visualizing this, they had to call to mind a color that they considered to be raw, harsh, and bright. This color represented the emotional tone of their conversation. Next, they imagined that, as they talked, the harsh tone of their conversation was mirrored in the background color in the room. They were then asked to imagine that the color softened all around them. Just as the harsh tone and light had represented their harsh conversation previously, as the color grew softer, so did their conversation. Although the meaning of the words they spoke to each other might be very similar or even identical in both scenes, the emotional tenor of the conversation was markedly different, and they could actually witness the difference because it was visible.

After participating in the exercise, they were asked to give an example of a recent argument. Then, they had to describe the color and quality of the light that they would use to illustrate their own part in the argument. The next time they got into a disagreement, they were assigned the task of "noticing" that the color of the conversation and speaking about it to each other. In subsequent sessions, both men reported that having this metaphor to help them discuss the emotional underpinnings of their conversations made it less likely that they would criticize each other in hurtful ways. The technique did not eliminate all unproductive conversation but was useful at times in curtailing personal attacks. When they could catch themselves being harsh with one another, they would discuss the color elements in their disagreements rather than continuing the harshness. Having another technique also helped them feel more empowered in attempting to come to terms with conflicts—as opposed to feeling overwhelmed and helpless, which had too often been their experience when trying to talk things out.

These guided-visualization exercises helped open the door for further exploration of the larger issue: what was preventing Mark and Rob from establishing themselves as a unified couple?

WHAT MAKES A COUPLE A COUPLE?

Developing confidence in one's ability to work toward the middle ground is enhanced for partners who visualize what this may feel and look like for them, within their own life situation *and* imagination. Mark and Rob had begun learning how to picture their movement forward together as a couple. To become more of a couple, they had to establish what this might mean for them.

What kind of a couple were they? Were they a "real" couple? A "pseudocouple"? A couple on their way to becoming "real" partners but not quite there yet? And what did these different couple designations mean? I felt that conversations needed to take place between myself and the men to help them establish a framework for evaluating their strengths and weaknesses as a couple. How could they move toward strengthening their status as a couple without a clearer under-standing of what was entailed?

So the question "What do couples do to establish themselves as couples?" was posed. For one, I responded, they transfer primary loy-alty to their partner. Neither family of origin nor a previous primary relationship can maintain place of primacy if the new partnership is to be *real*. Shifting the emotional center of gravity of one's life into a love partnership involves a commitment to resolving emotional issues rooted in the past.

In what would probably be the ideal scenario, a young person feels validated, understood, and appreciated for who he is by his parents. He also feels supported in his transition from being a member of the family to becoming a member of a new family through the creation of a partnership that, whether or not it includes having children, serves as the young person's new primary emotional home base. Loyalties to the family of origin are not expected to be severed, but the quality of attachment, up to this point primary, becomes reconfigured in the young person's life. The new family, the new home base, now assumes primacy. To let go of one's family of origin, it is important to have felt securely attached; this generally includes feeling that one is known, supported for being who one is, and free to move on. When young adults get the validation and encouragement that they need, they tend to feel more secure in making a definitive separation from their family of origin; you can think of it in terms of the firmness of a launching pad—the firmer the pad, meaning the more clearly defined and inte-grated one's connection with one's family, the more prepared one is to spring from those connections and form new ones, confident that the old ties may change but will not disintegrate.

When the sense of connection to family is less secure, less clear, the person will have a more difficult time giving up links to the past because the nature of the ties is mysterious and fragile. Because the past connections were poorly understood, the likelihood is that the act of making new connections will likewise be poorly understood. The whole business of connecting and demonstrating flexibility in transitioning from one set of connections to another will cause anxiety and confusion for a person who is leaving a situation where his or her role in relation to the family group has been poorly defined. The launching pad in this case can be thought of as mushy and affording little opportunity for a powerful send-off.

Mark had never had the benefit of feeling known by either of his parents. His father had died when he was quite young—as had Rob's father. Both fathers had been alcoholics. While living at home and during the time that he left home, Mark repeatedly attempted to engage his mother in conversations concerning his sexual identity; he wanted her to know who he was. Mark's mother managed to thwart any clear affirmation that she had "gotten the message" that he was gay. In other words, she continued, in her spoken understanding of who he was, to encourage him to think that he might outgrow his preference for male partners, and she "would not hear" that the choices he wished to make—the identity that he felt was authentic—centered on being accepted as a gay man. Before leaving home psychologically, he felt this task needed to be accomplished. That his mother blocked this accomplishment left him feeling that he was unable to psychologically leave home—he was haunted by a sense that unfinished business lay waiting for him to attend to and, until the issue was resolved, he felt thwarted in his attempt to have launched into the world.

Because he was not accepted as the man he was by his mother, he did not feel accepted or validated as a man. His mother's insistence that he did not know himself well enough to know this aspect of his identity clearly made him *feel* that, as far as she was concerned, he was not yet a man—seeing himself through his mother's eyes, he perceived a confused boy. He said, "I can live without feeling that she has come around to celebrate this part of who I am. The thing that rankles me, and hurts still, is that she actively denies this part of my identity. I know that it's a function of her own problems with it, but it still hurts and makes me feel inadequate for not being able to, at the very least, persuade her to open her eyes and see me for who I am. Rather than feeling like my break with her is in the past, her refusal to acknowledge who I am gives me an empty feeling, that something that should have been done, should have been finished, accomplished, may never get done. It bothers me. Sometimes I've caught myself doubting my own understanding about who I am. I've wondered, 'Am I really gay?' And then realized, like I was snapping out of a spell, that my identity as a gay man happens to be one of the few things in life that I am sure of. Nonetheless, that's how much her nonacceptance of my sexual identity has affected me. It causes me to feel confused about who I am."

In response to this theme in our work together, I coached Mark to write his mother a letter in which he described, in a nonblaming manner, the impact that her refusal to acknowledge his gayness has had on him. He had told me that it was important to him that he and his mother have a better understanding of how each felt about their lives and about the people with whom they felt connected. Mark stated in his letter that he had formed a relationship with Rob, that they were living together and trying to work out the kind of difficulties that couples who are committed to each other but argue too much and have complaints about their lives together go through. He told her that the reason he was including this information about Rob—whom his mother had never met and had never acknowledged as an important person in Mark's life—was because, in Mark's eyes, Rob had become a part of his family in the same sense that his sister's husband had become part of the family. It was not just because Rob was important to him that he wanted his mother to acknowledge their connection; it was, he explained, because *she* was so important to Mark that it felt sad or wrong that she should have no knowledge of someone who had become such a huge presence in his life and heart.

The writing of the letter was done in stages. Mark would write a draft of the letter and read it to me, and I would give him feedback about what he had written and suggest possible additions or changes. I asked Mark if he agreed with me that the letter should not be an instrument of venting but one that fostered new understanding. He agreed. This gave me an opportunity to speak at greater length about the term "middle ground" to Rob and Mark together; I described the idea of creating space within a relationship that was directed toward nonjudgmental communication, toward attempting difficult conversation in an atmosphere of safety for the purpose of resolving old hurts. They found the term helpful and began to use it in describing their own efforts to reach each other.

My feedback was geared to help Mark clarify his feelings and anticipate his mother's probable responses. In this way, Mark could both develop and monitor the empathic element in his communication with his mother; where I felt his anger at her resistance to acknowledging his gayness might be too overwhelming for her, I suggested that he tone down the language and focus on furthering the communication—keeping his mother in the dialogue—rather than indulging the desire to vent or, as in some of his earlier drafts of the letter, seek retribution for feeling misunderstood.

The letter-writing exercise is geared to benefit the writer regardless of the recipient's response. Because this technique—frequently used by family therapists—breaks down the steps in the communication process into distinct stages, it can be used as a primer on how to try to improve dialogue. Each stage can be used to focus on specific threads of dialogue. With Mark and Rob, we focused on the themes of empathy and self-acceptance.

As the recipient of his letter, Mark's mother was given the opportunity to hear her son's request for acknowledgement, and despite her history of repeated denials, she rose to the occasion. The letter moved her, and she was able to put aside her fundamentalist religious background and extend herself to him. She wrote, "If the Lord made it so clear to you [Mark] that this is the way you are, then there must be a purpose to it. He doesn't make mistakes." She discussed the letter with Mark's sister, Mark's elder by two years who had long known and accepted Mark's sexual identity. His mother, perhaps as a result of consulting with Mark's sister, concluded that Mark's persistence in attempting to get his core truth across to her was the right thing for him to have done. His mother, to Mark and Rob's surprise, wanted to meet Rob if they were inclined to come back home together. Rob, witness to the process as it unfolded, had gained much insight into Mark's struggle to free himself from his mother's negativism. It appeared that the letter-writing had created a middle ground between Mark and his mom, while strengthening the one that had been growing between Mark and Rob.

Rob's mother, by contrast, had been understanding and accepting of his sexual identity, but, although he had not known his father well, Rob harbored feelings throughout his life that if his father had been alive and a presence in his life, he would have disapproved. Rob had long ruminated over this anticipated rejection by his father, and it had depressed and pained him just as powerfully as if he had actually experienced it in direct interaction with his father.

I coached Rob to write a letter to his father in which he spoke about the feeling that his father disapproved of his gayness. With Mark looking on, Rob and I role-played a dialogue based on Rob's letter to his deceased father. I played the role of his father, and he read the letter to me. On one occasion, I role-played his father, and after he read the letter to me, I consoled Rob and assured him that I loved him deeply whether he was gay or straight. I expressed regret that I had not been able to live long enough to share more of Rob's life with him. On another occasion, in order to work through a different set of feelings toward his father and toward himself, I again role-played his father and was less accepting of Rob, less generous emotionally and essentially self-involved. When we discussed this interaction after the role-play, Rob stated that he derived satisfaction from having his thoughts and feelings responded to by his father, even if he was disappointed at his father's limitations.

"You know we'll never really find out what your father may have thought or felt about you being gay," said Mark, "but what I got from listening to the role-play was how important it was for Rob to accept himself and come to terms with the fact that if his father had been homophobic, it would not reflect on Rob's self-worth or his dignity— it would just be a shame that his father was so fucked up."

Rob nodded in agreement. Rob spoke about the real possibility that, in fact, his father would have been more accepting and generous with his emotions than Rob might have ever expected. Rob had been stuck ruminating about his father's rejecting attitude toward him for most of his life, an unquestioned belief that shaped a significant aspect of his attitude toward himself. This attitude had been challenged, however, by his experience with the letter-writing and role-playing, and his credence in this view—in which he was positioned as an object of scorn—had loosened and become subject for reexamination.

BALANCING THE "I" AND THE "WE"

For Mark and Rob, as with any couple that try to work through their difficulties, striking a balance in which the benefits of togetherness outweigh the sacrifices entailed by partnership is key. To maintain it favorably requires integrity and personal fortitude. Love alone is not enough.

Mark's long-term inability to achieve recognition of his sexual identity from his mother, as we have seen, tied him to her in a way that made it difficult for him to move on—to assume with confidence that he was capable of monitoring, modulating, and containing his emotions and identity—after all, according to his mother, he had been deemed incompetent to even identify his identity! He lacked confidence in his ability to emerge whole and intact from major relationship transitions—in his transition away from life at home to life in New York City on his own, he had felt frustrated since he'd been unsuccessful in establishing recognition of who he was while at home. Not only was this task still ahead of him, it was marked with a history of failure—his mother's denial set a negative precedent. Testing his mettle had taken on a negative cast because he had not had his mettle validated as real by his mother; that he had been "out" to his sister mitigated his mother's denial to some extent, but still, Mother's refusal to recognize him for who he was damaged and disorganized him. He had internalized her position like this: *whoever you are, you are certainly not someone who knows who he is*. A vote of confidence from home confirming his readiness to take a rightful place with his peers had not been cast. Support for his independent functioning as a maturing young man had been forcefully denied.

Our dialogue helped clarify how this affected Mark's ability to play a role in his relationship with Rob, which included making himself vulnerable to being known and to responding with love and patience to Rob's needs to be understood and cared for. Mark's "two-month or ten-meeting" rule spoke volumes on the subject. He had felt totally unprepared to be a loving partner. Though his relationship with Rob seemed to be an exception to these rules, the limitations that they imposed still resonated through Mark's thinking. Opening the relationship to other sexual partners increasingly seemed like it was a defensive maneuver designed to reinforce Mark's view of himself as incapable of being central to a loving partner and of giving and taking what was needed to keep the relationship alive.

By achieving some clarity concerning how and why his mother had found it impossible to get to know him, or—seen from a different vantage—until he could understand how she could be so incurious about what his true identity was, he seemed destined to remain stuck in a state of confusion and relational paralysis. His mother's shift in perspective, her acceptance of his identity as a gay man, though it did not solve all his difficulties instantly, gave him a sense of strength and satisfaction that allowed him to take positive steps in affirming his wish to remain bonded with Rob.

His earlier experiences with his mother—meaning her denial of his identity—had left him feeling that he was essentially either unknowable or not worth knowing! Either way, he had not been validated sufficiently to feel that achieving a mutual and intimate understanding of a partner was a realistic possibility for himself. This gives at least a partial account of the reasons that his mother's acceptance readied him to turn a corner and begin to entertain—although much of this went on at an unconscious level—possibilities that he might succeed at being known and knowing his partner. Similar comments might be used to describe the significance of Rob's breakthroughs in being able to question the fixity of his father's disapproval of his gayness.

Both Mark's and Rob's abilities to develop greater inner flexibility in evaluating possibilities for being accepted and/or understood contributed significantly to their ability to give to each other as partners. After all, "real" couples must demonstrate the ability to confer, cooperate, and communicate with one another about decisions that previously could be made autonomously, without any concern for another. In a "real" couple, partners must demonstrate the capacity to share intimate space when, at times, they might prefer time alone; in innumerable ways, they must demonstrate an openness to *knowing* the person they are with, to reading their own and their partner's needs, and to understanding the pattern of their own and their partner's personality. One might say that *real couples* do this sort of thing regularly and *pseudocouples* don't, won't, or can't.

Mark and Rob were, in this respect, making strides toward becoming a "real" couple. Also, partners like these men must learn to prioritize self-needs/other's needs/mutual needs in such a way as to honor each as fully as possible. Given the general busyness of contemporary life, this is no mean feat. This is an area that Mark and Rob had to negotiate over the entire course of my work with them. Their ability to find the time to have conversations, to have relaxation time, to have down time, to have time for sex, to spend some time socializing and some time with each other alone—coordinating all that developed a core of good feeling that enabled them to feel that they were sharing a life together. The pragmatics of joining the how, when, and where pieces that go into making togetherness a consistent force in a relationship can be—again, especially between two active and busy partners—as puzzling and difficult as a Rubik's cube. Talking over the problems involved and working out solutions on a step-by-step basis can change a pattern of bitterness to one of mutual accomplishment.

From the perspective laid out to this point, it may be clear that, depending on the maturity level of the partners, one or both may be unready to form a partnership. Yet another factor bears mentioning: *Couples can grow together*—as Mark and Rob did. And their wish to be connected helped each overcome deficits and reach out for the help they needed to feel not simply closer but more capable of experiencing closeness together. Partnership itself can spur interpersonal growth and psychological development. Therefore, couples, while lacking maturity, can enter a relationship with the need and wish to create a bond strong enough to carry them through a long-term relationship *and still succeed as a couple* if they can *grow* together—both individually and as a couple. Part of this growth often involves getting the necessary help to surmount obstacles to intimacy that crop up along the way. Close relationships offer challenges and require changes. So what may seem like a *pseudo*relationship may actually turn out to be a *budding relationship*, with the potential to develop into a deep, rich partnership.

Mark and Rob had no way to tell whether they could bring their relationship all the way back from the edge of despair, but they proved to have many of the ingredients that make success more probable than not. They had perseverance, a willingness to make themselves vulnerable to each other in talking through difficulties. They, like the couple who found their pink moon and sun, were poised to accept that, although there was much about each other they knew, there was much they did not, and, to recapture intimacy and trust, they would struggle to be open to learning. If your relationship is currently disappointing, there is no way to tell without trying everything within reason whether what you have is, or can become, so much more than it may seem. This was the outcome that Mark and Rob discovered.

COMMUNICATION TUNE-UP

Despite the breakthroughs, patterns of hostile communication still needed attention. Both men felt that their relationship had worsened since they had begun living together, but neither could explain why. Each described the other as distant for extended periods and admitted that their conversations were often caustic. A mix-up regarding the time and place of their arrangement for seeing a movie together had recently led to accusations and counterattacks. Rob blamed Mark's short temper and self-righteousness for this trend toward unfriendliness but did not exempt himself completely from responsibility. Mark was somewhat less generous in his assessment of who was at fault in the relationship's decline. He told me that Rob was not "stepping up" to do what was needed if they were going to feel close again. Rob acknowledged that they had "real problems with intimacy."

Mark quipped, "Problems with intimacy would be a step up for us. Maybe we should pencil that in as a goal. Right now, we are so far from intimacy that having problems with intimacy would be a gigantic accomplishment. What do you think, Rob? What we're working on is getting ourselves to be awake in the same room together. That's where we are now. We're at the dormant stage. Are we beyond help or what? What do you think?"

Though he expressed some real feeling, Mark's quiet laugh and Rob's snigger made clear that they could still share a laugh together. I wondered if the apparent good humor came out of recognition of shared frustration. Or had they given up on taking their pain seriously? I wasn't sure how to understand what was going on. So I asked Rob whether he felt that Mark's remarks were strictly for comic effect or if Mark had described a real problem in their life together.

WHEN LESS IS MORE

Rob replied, "It's funny and it's true. And then again it's not so funny. And I know that I'm guilty of being exhausted and more in need of recuperation than togetherness a lot of the time. That's real. I understand that. I work very hard. Probably too hard and too long. Mark works hard too though, and he sometimes is the one that is unreachable. I can tell you this for sure—I'm not the only one who has issues in this relationship."

> **Food for thought:** before reading further, take a moment to think about Rob's comment. There is an empathic element

in his communication—he acknowledges the point that Mark makes in his joke. What about his addition of, "I can tell you this for sure—I'm not the only one who has issues in this relationship"? It's as if the statement has two parts, and each serves a contradictory function. What are your thoughts about this style?

Mark responded to Rob's statement with anger. "You're not listening to me. You don't want to take in what I say. You just want to battle with me. I can't get my point across."

I commended Rob for acknowledging Mark's perspective—in the first part of his statement. This affords him and Mark a tenuous step into the middle ground. However, I cautioned Rob about acknowledging his partner's perspective and then—in the same breath, within the same statement—offering what amounts to a counterattack. The tail end of the statement—when Rob states that Mark created problems in their relationship, too—may well be true, but the *timing* is destructive. It undermines the middle-ground perspective. *Without* the add-on (retaliatory) remark, Rob's statement is nurturing and validating of Mark's internal experience; this is how and why it might foster mutuality, open middle ground. Going the extra—in my view, unnecessary—step and offering the countercriticism turns Rob's response into a classic example of not taking advantage of an opportunity for connection. *Less is more* sidesteps communication snags like this one. *Less* means leaving out the counterattack, and that adds up to *more* communication.

Some partners ask me, "Does that mean I have to think twice about everything I say? I want to feel like my communication is natural and direct. Having to endlessly analyze what I say and what my partner says takes all the spontaneity out of our being together."

Here is the way I respond: Certainly, you don't have to think twice about *everything* that you say, but when you *reflect* on what you say—which is what thinking twice really is, reflection on what you say or hear—it gives you an opportunity to raise your awareness of the effect that what you say has on your partner and the effect your partner's words have on you. If you resist *ever* taking this step, you won't realize that communication can be analyzed, which can yield newer, deeper, richer understandings about why certain ways of talking to each other are helpful and other ways may be harmful—all that is the work entailed in "working" on your relationship. Is it easy? Not always. But is relating unconsciously easy? Is confusion easy? Is a taboo against analyzing what is said and/or how you say things productive? The argument for not thinking about how communication unfolds because that cuts into spontaneity is a weak argument. After you analyze the communication, the things you learn become second nature; you no longer have to work at analyzing consciously, but you still benefit from having put that work into your relationship. Then you can be spontaneous *and* mindful at the same time! Without ever analyzing your communication somehow, you may be able to be spontaneous, but the mindful dimension will elude you. Mindfulness and reflection intertwine.

TURN-TAKING

Good communication often consists of taking turns. But turn-taking has to be understood in a particular way. Mark delivers a message; Rob's job is to receive and let his partner know that he's gotten it—before going on to his own message. This is how your partner can distinguish between when you are listening and when you are "marking time" for him to stop talking so that you can have your say. "Marking time" is a form of not-listening. Not-listening is unnerving to the person speaking.

Many speakers, when they sense that they are not being listened to, will either send their message again and again—sometimes louder and louder each transmission—or they will shut down and withdraw. Either way, the flow of communication ceases. Mark, who complained that Rob was not listening, is prone to repeating his message. This creates mutual resentment because Rob tires of hearing Mark repeat his message, and Mark is frustrated because he feels that Rob, because he gives no clear sign of having heard, makes it necessary for Mark to repeat himself. In addition, Mark resents that Rob takes no responsibility for having set the stage for his repetitions, so Mark feels Rob blames him for a situation brought about by Rob's irresponsibility—a vicious cycle.

The most important element in middle-ground dialogue is its reciprocity. For any statement to receive its due, it must be articulated, then processed and returned to the sender with an indication that it has been heard. If this is short-circuited or interrupted by the addition of extraneous information, the process is either stalled or diluted.

The idea of *slowing down* communication so that understandings can be established—through explicit statements that validate that messages have been received—often sounds abstract to couples. Slowing down doesn't mean talking slower—it has to do with slowing down *reactivity*; layering reflection into communication often can be achieved by deliberately adding interim steps to the process. These steps create a *pause in the action* during which partners *acknowledge* and/or *appreciate* what their partner has said to them. Numerous communication exercises included in this book can take you through this process in step-by-step procedures that can be used as a template for improving how you and your partner talk together.

> **Food for thought:** Do you and your partner take turns communicating? Do you demonstrate you've heard what your partner has said and then in the next breath send back a volley of your own concerns, as Rob did? There is a basic form for accomplishing communication that rarely comes intuitively to those of us who did not grow up in an environment that fostered open emotional communication. This form generally involves accomplishing one piece of communication at a time. Trying to do too much ends up with accomplishing little or nothing. Can you recall conversations that went awry because they continued for too

long? This happens between partners frequently. How can you begin to do this if you have never done this before? This is the purpose of the communication exercises included in the book. They provide basic forms that facilitate communication and enhance clarity and emotional safety in communication. By practicing the exercises, you get a chance to see what collaborative communication feels like. Describing it for you can help you think about it, but there is no substitute for actually experiencing these middle-ground exercises. They create a safety net around conversation that maximizes possibilities for resolving hot issues and deescalating anger. Practice will not make perfect. Perfect is not the point. Practice will make for good enough, and that is what we are aiming for here. Good enough to allow for meaningful communication and emotional safety.

REACHING FOR POSITIVES

I asked Mark if he ever experienced his parents talk through differences or resolve a conflict in a way that might be helpful for him to implement with Rob. He said he would think about the question but couldn't come up with anything right then.

Approaching Rob in a similar vein, I asked if he, as a child, had any experience witnessing adults work through their problems in a way that he felt had been constructive. Since he had grown up without knowing his father, I was hoping to get a feeling for whether he and his mother felt isolated. I wondered if there were any other adult figures involved in the household.

Rob said his Aunt Lilly lived in the same building as he and his mom and that she often visited and participated in activities with them. She and his mother could talk over things and make cooperative decisions, and Aunt Lilly provided a bridge between him and his mom and others in important ways. He had vivid memories of when Aunt

Lilly—a mother of two girls, his favorite cousins—would occasionally come over and help his mother rearrange furniture. They would often make an evening of it, both becoming enthusiastic about trying out various design ideas; then, seated on one of the two comfortable chairs in the living room, with an index finger riding across her top lip, thumb tucked under her chin and one eye half shut as if a sharpshooter adjusting her sights so as to hit a distant bull's-eye, Lilly would pronounce her verdict on the new order: "It's okay, but I think I like the dresser better over there." Or "I don't know what I was thinking, but it doesn't work." Or then Mom might say, "Now that's more like it! What do you think?"

Rob said, "Aunt Lilly gave us an aura of community. Mom wasn't raising me all by herself. And Aunt Lilly was like a mother to me as well. She made a big difference in my life."

I was excited that I had found something in Rob's history that smacked of mutuality and was meaningful to him. I asked Mark if he had any relatives who had become a part of his immediate family in this way. Mark said the only model for external helpfulness he could think of was when the delivery guys brought pizza on time. But then he added, "The only bright spot was between me and my sister. Without her, I don't think I'd have even made it through." So each man, though feeling emotionally deprived in many ways, both growing up without a father or a father figure in the home, had experienced kindness and cooperation in their formative years. This was a hopeful discovery.

Mark seemed to be quite inspired by Rob's description of Aunt Lilly. It was as if Rob, under the full glare of the spotlight and after having demonstrated to all that there was nothing hidden up his sleeves, had pulled a white rabbit out of his hat. She was something of a revelation to all three of us. Although Rob's mother was warm and supportive at times, in previous conversation, his home life had seemed quite bleak, and he conveyed the impression that his mother was alone and forlorn much of the time they were together. A same-sex buddy who had beautified his home and lightened his mother's life with the gift of companionship, Lilly enriched the men's heritage in much the way a gorgeous heirloom might have enhance an otherwise barren space. Lilly and Mark's sister, Joanna, became a point of reference on numerous occasions throughout our work together. They constituted proof that—at least in certain respects and in spite of their hardships—although things certainly could have been better for each in their childhoods, things also could have been worse. Each had some foundation for understanding a sense of gratitude for what they had in their lives. And this feeling was going to grow.

Chapter 4

OLDER CAN BE BETTER

Cassie entered the office with a series of quick strides and made a beeline for the seat closest to the window. Her hair was light brown, rather short, layered on top with short fringy bangs resting on her forehead. She carried herself with a youthful, casual elegance that, at sixty-eight, intimated that she felt comfortable with how she presented herself. She wore a sky-blue silk shirt above a pair of dark slacks and carried a large bag, almost satchel size, that signaled preparedness for any contingency.

Max, her senior by seven years, matched her style points. His tan fedora was set at a slightly rakish angle; his multicolored tie, festive and tasteful, brought out the rich chocolate of his Western-style vest. The subtly iridescent raincoat tossed over his left shoulder seemed to call for a jauntier stride than the one he managed. His demeanor also clashed with his wardrobe choices. His facial expression was neither carefree nor weary-wise, just careworn and weary—hangdog. "Less Sinatra than Bert Lahr," I thought then wondered, "Why am I thinking Bert Lahr? Is there a cowardly lion lurking? Do the clothes fit the man or disguise him?"

Another seemingly random question flitted to mind: How would

Max look if he were seated in the windowless corner of a restaurant noted for its scenic views? And this mental picture led me to surmise: He would look just the way he does right now. Does he feel shoved in the corner here? I wondered about this. How much stock did I put in these internal musings of mine? Not much at this point, but then again, I had no reason to dismiss them out of hand. Perhaps I was picking up or tuning into something?

Cassie set about making herself comfortable, adjusting the throw pillows. She had me shut the air conditioner with an off-hand command, "Too cold in here. Shut the air down, would you?"

With the room temperature adjusted, she glanced over toward Max and told him to stop fussing with his hat. She then locked eyes with me momentarily and said, "He looks like a nice old man, doesn't he? But you know what he is? He's a torturer. That's what he is, and I'm the one he keeps in his dungeon. Do you hear what I'm saying?"

She looked at me as if she weren't sure I spoke English. "He's sweet and charming, and everybody loves Doctor Max, but do you know something? They don't know him the way I do. And you know what, they're lucky."

They had been married fourteen years. I wondered how long she'd felt this way. An eminent researcher and practitioner, John Gottman stated that one of the main reasons couples' therapy failed, when it did, was that couples wait too long before seeking help. The average wait is, according to his research, six years. I hoped that Max and Cassie had not waited too long.

Although her words were unambiguous, I wasn't sure *how* to interpret them. Was she being theatrical? Or expressing the way she felt accurately? Was he the cause of her misery or was she in misery and using him as a scapegoat? Max subtly rearranged his position on the couch, leaning away from the window side of the room where Cassie sat. Max cleared his throat but said nothing. He then chuckled almost breathlessly and smiled in her general direction. His look was full of reproof, as if he were a naughty boy and she a tattletale.

Cassie continued. "What we have here is two people who live

together but don't share a life. If he took care of me the way he takes care of his patients, I wouldn't be complaining."

Cassie and Max had been introduced sixteen years earlier by a mutual friend. That was two years after Irene, his wife of thirty-eight years, mother of his three sons, had been diagnosed with an incurable cancer and perished within months of the determination, and it was one year after Irene's death. Cassie had been gainfully employed as executive secretary/office manager at a Wall Street firm for many years prior to meeting Max. After his receptionist/office manager of many years retired, she helped out and was instrumental in keeping his office organized and functional. She quickly became the lynchpin of his professional and personal life.

MAX'S PATH TO CASSIE

Max's marriage to Irene had not been terribly unhappy, but neither had it been joyful. Over time the two grew distant. She, preoccupied with raising the children and he, absorbed with his medical practice, became like houseguests in each other's home. Each kept a keen eye on the demands of the moment, rarely on each other. The episodic journey from the way they had been as a young couple to the way they were as empty nesters seemed of a piece. For Max, the time vanished mysteriously, thousands of mundane rituals like dressing and shaving piled up, multiplied by their concordant number of minutes and seconds until they equaled decades. Somehow this gigantic skein of ordinary moments arranged in sequential order—like a slow pan from engine to caboose—had been assembled. But to Max at least, no climax or resolution had been implied. The train just kept moving on, and he was not in the habit of thinking about how or why. Such questions were foreign to his temperament and mind-set. Until, with great suddenness, the train jerked to a stop and unceremoniously dumped him and Irene out.

Disembarking in middle age, they no longer knew who they were to one another. Max wondered how and why they had grown so far apart. He also wondered how close they had ever been. His thoughts, ordinarily filled with routine medical and business practicalities, now buzzed with the unanswerable, questions he'd typically consider a waste of time—about time itself. How had it affected him and his life? The relentless flow of time, punctured by middle age, had been savagely punctuated with the quick twist her illness brought.

The youngest of his three sons had married and left the house less than a hundred days before Irene's illness was discovered. Max grieved but also felt guilty about feeling more dazed than bereft. To him, Irene was not so much a part of him that had withered but an example of how nature and the world operate unfeelingly. Her death underscored his own vulnerability. Max felt that he had not been as present and involved a father as his boys were due, but Irene had covered for him so well. He had reasoned that she took good care of all parental functions. Of course, she could not give them a father's love, but she did her best to assure them that Daddy was an important part of the efforts and concern that she expended in their behalf. With Irene gone though, Max would have to reconfigure his relationship with his sons, and, though others might not realize how hard this would be, he felt ill-prepared to meet the challenge. He fell into a depression soon after Irene's funeral. Those around him took it as a sign of grief. He pushed himself through his days, holding up but shaken. Without having paid much conscious attention to sorting out his identity for so long, he now entered the realm of identity in crisis.

This was when Cassie became important to him. She listened patiently as he spilled out his confused thoughts and feelings. She could rise to the occasion and curtail any gruffness in her Brooklyn-bred manner. He felt he had never spoken so openly to anyone before. Perhaps, he remembered having thought, he had never needed to. He had never felt lost like this before. He never had been.

His listener confirmed that his feelings made sense to her. Yes, she said, she could understand how difficult it would be, how confusing it would be, to experience Irene's loss, particularly the suddenness of it, in just the way he had experienced it. There were many other reassuring conversations. A tender understanding developed in Max. He understood that she understood him. And for this, as well as other reasons, he began to feel deeply attached to this woman, who became his second wife and now sat before me, complaining.

CASSIE'S PATH TO MAX

Unlike Max, who was the youngest of three children, Cassie had been an only child. She had grown up in an atmosphere of continuous rancor and dissension. Her father was employed by his brother in a factory in the garment district in Manhattan, and that relationship was a source of ongoing competition and bad feeling that spilled from the workplace into the home. Cassie's mother, a first-generation American whose family had emigrated from Eastern Europe, was unable to stand up for herself against her father's continuous tirades. Her father drank immoderately and gambled away much of the family's scarce resources.

Cassie excelled in school but was tracked into what was called a commercial diploma. Although her competence was recognized, she was encouraged, as many women of that day were, to aim no higher than for secretarial work. After she graduated from high school, Cassie met Bruce while working part-time in a summer position as a temp. He was four years older than she and pursued her. She enjoyed his attention at first, but the feeling never blossomed into anything she would have described as love. He established himself as a presence in her life, brought her gifts, and ingratiated himself to her parents. Within the first eight weeks of their seeing each other, Bruce committed what would, in this time, be judged as an egregious example of date rape. Although she felt brutalized and angered by the experience, as she tells the story, she was so desperate to leave her parents' home that, when he offered to marry her to "make right" what had happened, she consented.

The marriage, the only one that Cassie experienced before meeting Max, was loveless and strained. Cassie was an extremely competent worker and threw herself into her work. Shortly after their marriage, Bruce began drinking heavily and having affairs. Although divorce was much less common at that time, the relationship was terminated after three years of disharmony. Before meeting Max, so many years later, Cassie neither planned nor expected to remarry.

PRESENTING PROBLEMS

Cassie had accused Max of being her torturer. I asked her what he had done.

"What he did is that he married me, but he didn't really marry me. He's still married to his work. There has to be more to what we have than what we've got." It sounded a little strange, but then I realized she had said something quite profound, worthy of Yogi Berra in his prime. *There's got to be more to what we have than what we've got.* In other words, there's got to be a way for us to redeem the value of what we have so that it becomes worth much more than what we are experiencing together at the moment.

I asked Max what he thought of what Cassie had said. "What she's saying is not completely true, but it's more true than not." I asked him to clarify further, "Which part of what she said is true?"

"She wants me to stop working, and then when we discuss it, she agrees that in order to do the things that we like to do, it makes sense for me to keep working. So she wants me to be with her, but she understands why I'm still working." He paused. "Then again, she'll tell you that I take my work home with me and haven't been with her in the way that it seemed I was going to. She may be right about that. I don't know. What do you think? You're the expert on relationships."

I had three hypotheses about why Cassie might dilute the pressure she had been applying to get Max to retire. One had to do with a possible internal conflict she had regarding whether she was entitled to have what she really wanted. Another had to do with her feeling frightened that if she did get her wish, unanticipated difficulties might cause unforeseen stress and disappointment. The other possibility was that Max was misrepresenting what she said. This led to a discussion of their finances and to a mutual recognition by the partners that, in fact—because Max had worked continuously as a physician for over forty years *and* Cassie had resources of her own as well—they could enter a full or part retirement status whenever they decided.

Responding to Max's question about my relationship expertise, I said, "Okay, it seems to me that there is a lot of pressure built up in your relationship, and before being able to commit yourselves to making any major changes, you both would benefit from listening very closely to how you each feel about what is going on for each of you individually and as marital partners. It seems like in the beginning of the relationship, you had developed a very close understanding of each other and that you are now struggling to reconnect. Cassie, you've said that you feel alone in the marriage. Max, do you feel this way also? Does that seem accurate for you? Does it make sense to you?" I made eye contact with both partners.

At this point, we began to work with the two exercises immediately following this chapter—"One Talks, the Other Doesn't" and "Reaching Out from the Inside." Using these exercises and then discussing the content that emerged from them made a number of underlying issues more comprehensible to both partners.

WHAT WE DISCOVERED

I worked with Max, using the communication exercises that follow this chapter, to explore his indecisiveness in regard to slowing down and/or curtailing his practice. He was able to articulate that he was frightened about acknowledging to himself that he was indeed entering a new phase of his life. He said that if he could forestall his retirement, he *felt* that he could in some way forestall the aging process itself. Sometimes, and this proved to be relevant to what happened with Max at this point in our work, given the opportunity to "think out loud," he could evaluate his own thinking with increased objectivity. He was able, using the process formalized in the "One Talks, the Other Doesn't" exercise, to change perspective. For example, when he heard himself saying that by delaying retirement, he might delay aging and ultimately keep death itself at bay, this brought his scientific sensibility to bear on these irrational thoughts and feelings. He literally laughed out loud and commented, "I counsel my patients to plan and act sensibly regarding their own retirement issues, yet here I am, thinking that some kind of magical thinking is going to deter the forces of nature."

Other discussions on this topic prior to Max's sitting down with Cassie resulted in a planned phasing out of his medical practice. Their discussion of the issue, as a topic that demanded their attention, was confirmed as open and active. This was an important step toward formulating a plan for their life together after Max's retirement.

OTHER ASPECTS OF HEALING

Prior to coming in to talk about their problems, Cassie would bring up issues—often related to his working too much—and he would deflect them. If he wasn't too tired or hungry or exhausted, he would slip away from the possibility of a substantive conversation by labeling her approach as hostile. Then he'd begin name calling. Because Cassie wanted to raise these issues, he'd call her a nag, a downer, a broken record, and so on. The capital of goodwill that they had accumulated at the beginning of their relationship had dwindled from the black to the red. The mood of the relationship had progressively grown colder. Max became increasingly defensive in Cassie's presence. And she felt more and more abandoned, betrayed, angry, frustrated, and—as she had put it—tortured.

We discussed what it might mean that Max would call her these names—given what we had learned about Max's underlying fears connected to retirement and aging, in the past, he had been frightened and unable to respond. Now that he had gained awareness of these underlying feelings, Cassie could develop a new understanding of what she had taken to be his rejecting and unfriendly manner. He said, "I apologize not only because it [the name calling] was the wrong thing to do but especially because I now realize that I was hurting you, and I really don't want to do that." The middle ground was expanding. Cassie saw that she had gotten her point across and that Max had accepted, acknowledged, and responded to her feelings. Some of her bitterness dissolved.

They began to schedule more activities together on the weekends. Interestingly enough, Cassie gradually became more trusting and was able to confide in Max that she was having physical difficulties. She had been ignoring the problems because they frightened her. Just as he had been ruled by a silent, unacknowledged fear of death, Cassie had felt unable to face up to having a physical examination because she was terrified about having her worst fears confirmed. Certainly Max understood this situation well; it mirrored his own difficulty coming to terms with his fears in so many ways. He was, during our session time, able to follow the steps of the "Reaching Out from the Inside" exercise and assure her that he indeed understood what she was going through. He paraphrased her description of it, using much of her own language, and spelled out his understanding of how uncomfortable those nagging fears were. He made clear that he had a firm grasp on what she had told him about avoiding medical examinations for fear of finding out she was ill. Her previous inability to share these feelings with Max had epitomized a way in which Cassie had felt alone and isolated with her difficulties in their marriage. She now felt that she could go to Max for comfort that previously had seemed impossible. She had helped him cope. Now he reciprocated. He was able to be reassuring. She was able to allow herself to be comforted. The middle ground was becoming deeper and richer.

Other elements entered into the work that I did with Max and

Cassie. There were explorations of their early lives, their relationships with their parents and grandparents. There was, as there always is, intergenerational transmission of both strengths and difficulties. As the work progressed, Cassie spoke of feeling resigned, for most of her adult life, to the probability that she would never be in a caring relationship with a man. Her previous experience with men—mirrored in her understanding of her mother and father's relationship—had been that women made a choice to either resist involvement with a man or surrender their individuality. She felt that with Max, she had the chance to both fall in love with him and still be able to preserve her sense of self. Then, when he grew distant and unreachable, unwilling to clear time to share a life with her, she felt so bitterly angry that she revealed that she, at times, had contemplated suicide. Stunned, Max—at this point, he was sitting next to her on the couch—said, "I am so sorry. And at the same time, I'm so glad that you're here. And so glad that you are telling me this. If you had ever done that, I believe it would have destroyed me."

She turned to him tearfully and said, "Thank you for saying that." She paused. "Just so you know, I never would have done it. Never. But I did think about it. I felt that bad. But I never would do that." Max kissed her gently on the cheek.

It was clear that they had weathered a lot of pain and loneliness but now had become rejoined.

Another major area of middle-ground work involved Max's efforts to improve Cassie's connection to his sons' families. Cassie, in part because of the difficulties she had experienced with Max, felt only marginally included in the larger family. This problem had been acknowledged between Max and Cassie, but no solution had been put into effect. In Cassie's presence, I worked with Max to help him approach his sons and see if he could enlist their help in changing the situation. This resulted in numerous father-son talks that went in an interesting but not altogether predictable direction. Max came to realize that he and his sons had never spoken about their feelings related to their mother's death. The sons—Charles, Benjamin, and

Peter—each in different ways and to varying degrees had a lot of unresolved feelings, and sharing these with their father appeared to
strengthen their sense of unity as a family. The suddenness of their
mother's death had been so jarring that they had resisted accepting that
this chapter of their life had to be closed. Accepting Cassie more fully
may have signified to them that they would be cut off from memories
of their mother or that their allegiance to their mother might be diluted
somehow. The precise workings of the psychological alchemy that
these father-son talks produced is difficult to track, but the upshot was
that Cassie began to feel more welcomed and included into the family
circle. She was thrilled about the increased involvement with her six
lovely grandchildren.

EXERCISE: ONE TALKS, THE OTHER DOESN'T

A Basic Stretch to Promote Safe Stretching

This exercise can help you create a personal benchmark and empower
you to distinguish between risking too much—stretching too far—and
challenging yourself appropriately. Large increments in the intensity
or duration of our stretches—think of yoga, for example—not only
cause injury but frequently discourage us continuing to exercise. How
do you gauge yourself? How do you pace yourself? And when you are
exercising your ability to share what you are feeling, how do you do it
in a graduated fashion? That's what this exercise is about. Avoid doing
too much or starting too fast. On the other hand, get started and guard
against using the fear of injury to rationalize doing nothing.

Nuts and Bolts

Content of communication: When beginning this exercise, limit communication to neutral or uncontroversial topics. Later, pressing matters can be explored. *The speaker's emphasis must be on self-explo-*

ration and not on blaming or assigning guilt. Anger can be discussed from an inside-out perspective ("I-statement") in which the speaker describes her internal experience of anger and connects it to external trigger points. Explore how these trigger points bring on feelings— with the emphasis and focus on understanding the emotion.

Length of communication: At first, communication should be five minutes or less per turn. Once you and your partner are more familiar with the procedure, each turn can increase gradually up to ten minutes per individual turn. Time limits should be prearranged; however, if one speaker wishes to stop before the limit is up, that must be accepted.

Frequency of exercise: The exercise should be used three or four times per week for a period of at least three weeks. At that point, based on responses to the experience, it can be continued as needed. Some couples find this exercise useful when trying to deal with communicating particularly difficult feelings or ideas. A partner can call "time out" in the midst of an argument that feels unproductive and suggest that, rather than continue arguing, they engage in a round of this structured talk. This can bring down anger levels dramatically and, potentially, put the discussion back on course. This exercise and the "Reaching Out from the Inside" exercise (the next section in this chapter) can work well in alternating sequence.

Procedure

Step One: One partner speaks *as if* she or he were alone while in the presence of the other. The speaking partner has the opportunity to present thoughts verbally and to develop themes and associations without fear of interruption or interference.

Listener, you do not respond verbally. The Listener's function is simply to "be there" to contain, as witness, whatever the speaker says. The Listener is a gigantic human ear. Nothing more or less. The goal is for each partner to expose thoughts and feelings in the presence of the other without having to contend with any interference or competition. Because the Listener does not comment on the Speaker's words, the influence of the Listener on the Speaker is minimized. The Speaker can focus attention on the manner in which she experiences herself in the act of identifying and expressing her own thoughts and feelings.

This is a unique opportunity to sort internal from external influences.

Note: the Speaker may choose to bring up topics discussed in this exercise at other times, but unless the Speaker chooses to do so, the Listener must agree not to initiate conversation concerning anything the Speaker divulges during this exercise.

Because the Listener does not respond openly to the Speaker's statements, the Speaker cannot use the Listener's responses to gauge the direction or content of what is said. The Speaker is encouraged to notice anytime she might feel herself avoiding expressing what she is thinking or feeling. In this sense, what is not said, if noted, can yield valuable information for the Speaker as well. In the absence of the Listener's active influence on the flow of the Speaker's line of expression, the Speaker is free to reflect on the extent to which she is aware of monitoring, extending, modifying her expressions during *ordinary* discourse with her partner. These tendencies can be thrown into high relief as a result of the contrast between ordinary discourse and this structured interaction. The structure of the exercise supports the Speaker's ability to remain attuned to following the line of her own thoughts and feelings as accurately as possible.

For many, this combination—feeling connected *and* having some control—is highly unusual. All of this provides crucial learning and growing experience for individuals in couples and for couples as a unit.

Step Two: Partners exchange roles. The Speaker becomes the Listener and vice versa, and the process repeats.

Learning about Feelings

Attaining a grasp of the realness of one's feelings is certainly a precondition for active and meaningful dialogue between partners. This is a skill that can't be taken for granted.

Nurturing partners' ability to identify and acknowledge their emotions in each other's presence can be instrumental to furthering interpersonally connected dialogue. Couples can use this exercise to practice and strengthen these skills.

Between Public and Private

Using this exercise, partners express private thoughts and feelings publicly—in the presence of their partner—but still insulated from the realm of discussion. Why is this important? Because it validates an area in which you or your partner can have your thoughts validated by the presence of the other but still remain wholly your own. Some partners have never been able to share in this way. Many parents do not provide such a space for their children; as a result, not having been given a chance to hear themselves think out loud, many have trouble, odd as it may seem, figuring out what they are in fact thinking. This exercise zeroes in on this subtle but important need.

Although thinking before speaking is a good communication goal, there is a developmental stage during which a child needs to feel free to express herself without feeling censored. First, speech must be developed, the function integrated, then shaped, and, if you will, edited. Those who were never supported in producing a full flow of their own language benefit greatly from this exercise.

Taking turns speaking to each other *without* commenting in any way on what has been said fortifies this layer of middle ground, which, for many couples, provides a unique experience. This often creates a sense of intimacy between partners—a shared experience of mutual respect and accommodation that carries over into other dialogues.

Safer Arguments

This exercise is also effective at creating an island of conversational safety for couples who argue too much. It provides a highly structured safe space in which both partners can anticipate having each other's attention and the opportunity to express themselves. Premium on feeling safe and in control is reemphasized for the Speaker *and the Listener*—as roles are understood by both partners as interchangeable.

EXERCISE: REACHING OUT FROM THE INSIDE

Most couples experiencing communication problems live with the feeling that their partner is not "really listening" to what they say, not able to or not interested enough to get their message. This exercise addresses this predicament.

You speak and your partner listens. Your partner then tells you what he's heard, and you confirm that he's gotten the message or hasn't.

The exercise gives you an opportunity to confirm that the message you have intended to send has been received as you intended it.

The method fosters each partner's ability to see things from the other's point of view. Use it with the Basic Three-Step. This procedure can halt the escalation of anger when "hot" topics are discussed.

> **Key point:** The structure of the exercise prohibits either partner from competing with the other's point of view. Each partner gets access to the other's point of view, and the potential for mutuality within the relationship is reinforced.

Couples' therapists make wide use of this core communication exercise. Pat Love and Jo Robinson in their book *Hot Monogamy* describe a similar exercise process that they call "Mirroring." They discuss its value in encouraging couples to differentiate from each other. Howard Markman, noted couples' therapist, calls another variation of this method the "Speaker-Listener Technique" in his book *Fighting for Your Marriage*; there, he emphasizes, as I do, its usefulness in cooling off heated conversation.

Starting to Use the Exercise

When you begin to use the exercise, topics of communication should not be *controversial* so that the form of the exercise becomes familiar and clear to you and your partner. After the method is familiar, more difficult issues can be introduced. The exercise ultimately is helpful in approaching problematic issues but can also be used to help couples communicate good feelings.

Procedure

I have broken the process into five steps. Throughout this sequence, one partner remains the Speaker, and the other is the Listener. After the sequence is completed, the partners exchange roles.

The Speaker maintains the floor until he feels satisfied that the essential message or train of thought has been conveyed *or* a pre-arranged time limit has been reached, whichever comes first. At first, limit the exercise to three minutes a turn. After becoming more familiar with the process, time can extend to five, seven, or ten minutes per turn. If the exercise feels emotionally unsafe at home, it is a good bet that you and your partner would benefit from trying it in the presence of a couples' therapist.

1. *Speaker sends message to Listener.* The partners face each other in a comfortable seated position that allows easy eye contact. The Speaker addresses the Listener in clear sentences, using Basic Three Step-statements and avoiding blame, name calling, or any other form of verbal attack. The Speaker conveys his point in deliberately short units, a few sentences in length.
2. *The Listener paraphrases the Speaker's point.* The Listener paraphrases the Speaker's point and asks whether it was captured accurately. The Listener responds with calm expression throughout. The Speaker confirms whether his message has

been received accurately by the Listener. If the Speaker feels the point has not been grasped, he is expected to describe that something has been omitted, misinterpreted, deemphasized, or overemphasized and restate the original message, with emphasis on the aspect that had been missed. If the Speaker feels his message has not been accurately paraphrased, this must be communicated calmly.

3. *After confirming the Listener's paraphrase, the Speaker continues to build his statement or train of thought.* The Listener signals readiness to listen further by nodding head while making eye contact or saying, "Uh-huh" or "Go on" or asking, "Is there more?"

4. *The Listener paraphrases the Speaker's elaboration, and the Speaker responds as in step 2.* This process continues until the Speaker feels the statement is complete and has been received or until a prearranged time limit is reached.

5. *The Speaker and the Listener then exchange roles, and the process begins again.* Turns should be of approximately equal length. If time length becomes unbalanced, using a timer can help.

A Live Illustration

SPEAKER: I feel at a loss. I feel angry and helpless when we discuss how we are going to share household responsibilities. Somehow, it seems like you want or expect me to change things that have already happened. *[Initial statement.]*

LISTENER *[attempts to paraphrase]*: You're saying that you feel that I am focused on the past and that this makes you feel helpless. Is that right?

SPEAKER: That's right *[confirms that first part of message has been received before continuing]*. I have accepted responsibility for mistakes I have made, and it seems that no matter what I say, we can't seem to move past these problems. *[First elaboration.]*

LISTENER: You feel that you've accepted responsibility for mistakes and also feel that the problems do not go away. *[Attempt to paraphrase.]*

SPEAKER: That's not it exactly. It's more than that they don't go away. It's like I don't feel like we make any headway with them. It's like we've never discussed it before, even though we've been over it many times. *[Speaker asks for Listener to amend paraphrase.]*

LISTENER: So you feel it's more than that the problems don't go away. It's like you feel that no progress is made toward improving the situation. Is that it? *[Listener amends paraphrase.]*

SPEAKER: Yes, that's it. That's exactly how I feel *[Speaker confirms amended paraphrase]*. I'm not saying that we don't have work to do. What I'm saying is that I'd like to feel that there's some movement in a positive direction. I feel very frustrated, as if whatever I say just disappears into a void and doesn't get acknowledged. I don't know how to say these things differently, in a way that will make a difference. *[Speaker offers new section.]*

LISTENER: You feel that you know that there are still problems to work on and you accept that but that you are very frustrated because you don't see our efforts going anywhere, making a difference. *[Paraphrase.]*

SPEAKER: Yes. That's it. *[Paraphrase confirmed.]*

At this point, the Speaker and the Listener exchange roles, and the former Listener becomes the Speaker and uses the identical method to discuss an issue of her choosing—not continuing with the same issue that the first Speaker brought up. The reason is that it gives the exercise a feeling that it is a structured debate. It is not. It is a structured method for ensuring that listening occurs. The focus is on promoting the feeling that each partner has been understood—indeed, that communication, painstaking as it may be at times, is possible.

One Important Benefit

The beauty of this exercise is that it *slows down* the dialogue so that one issue at a time can be dealt with. The technique can conserve a sense of emotional safety so that topics that might otherwise be impossible to approach can be talked about. Not everyone is a fan of this exercise. Couples sometimes complain that the method feels stilted. To couples likely to benefit most from this method, nearly any communication that is not a form of belligerence will tend to feel stilted. Angry dialogue can become habit-forming. Other forms of talk, to couples with an advanced anger habit, may feel unnaturally constrained. Stilted, in this context, becomes highly recommended. If you experience high anger levels in your current conversations, I recommend stilted. Aim for stilted.

Chapter 5

PARENTHOOD

NOTE

This chapter is divided into two sections. The first focuses on problems related to parenting a youngster with what is called "special needs," which often translates into having a need for an individualized education program. In the second section, the focus shifts to problems that develop between partners as a result of directing virtually all their emotional energy toward nurturing their child(ren) and at the expense of neglecting their partner.

SECTION 1: PARENTING A "SPECIAL NEEDS" CHILD

Intercultural, interfaith, interracial, the union of Isabelle and Kevin was a showcase of diversity. The spread of connections and attachments that could be linked to their respective backgrounds was the subject of conversation and wonderment among many who knew them. He had been born in Barbados and then moved to the streets of East Harlem during his late teens. His countenance included the high cheek bones and deep-set eyes of remote Thai forbears, which, when joined with his large dark eyes, well-proportioned nose, and full mouth, brought an association of Bob Marley to mind when we were introduced; Mayan lineage added yet another exotic cast to his face. Depending on the eye of the beholder, Kevin personified a classic example of a young man from the "islands" or, to others, perhaps an international citizen—more from everywhere than anywhere in particular.

Isabelle's mother's roots were a blend of Eastern European and Sephardic Jew. Her mother's sparkling blue eyes and tightly wound, honey-colored curls were evident in Isabelle's appearance. From her father, she was bequeathed a lean physique, a stringent work ethic, a gift for mathematics and a love of poetry. Both her parents were second-generation Americans. Her father identified himself as a nonobservant Roman Catholic and derived from Scotch–Irish–German ancestry.

Isabelle and Kevin reported difficulties with their seven-year-old son, Jaime, at our first meeting. Jaime had been described as "somewhat overactive, easily distracted, too often daydreaming in class." His second grade teacher, Ms. Bonner, had—a week prior to Isabelle and Kevin's first meeting with me—complained that Jaime was not handing in classroom assignments and too often ignoring her directions and instructions in class. When Ms. Bonner attempted to redirect him back to on-task activities and behavior, Jaime often did not respond cooperatively. Isabelle quoted the teacher: "He's not exactly defiant but lags behind his peers in terms of picking up on social cues." Despite his difficulties, Jaime could grasp the basic academic concepts presented. The teacher's concern seemed to be not so much that he was behind his classmates academically but that, if his off-task behavior continued, he might fall behind.

Isabelle had also been told that Jaime spoke of an imaginary friend, a puppy who he said kept company with him, usually by hiding under his desk at school. Upon hearing this, Isabelle had become upset, but after discussing the puppy with Jaime, she was reassured to learn that Jaime readily acknowledged that the puppy was "only make-believe." Still Jaime insisted, "He is make-believe but a good friend."

Isabelle tearfully admitted that she felt guilty about Jaime's difficulties. She questioned whether she had been lax in disciplining him and felt responsible for his difficulty in acting in accordance with his teacher's guidelines. We explored the issue further, and I asked her to give me an example in which she felt she had failed to provide assistance or direction or to explain or enforce proper boundaries for Jaime. She described a situation in the playground where she intervened quickly when Jaime got into an argument with a playmate to ensure that he "use his words" and not have the disagreement turn into a physical fight. It seemed to me that she had done an admirable job of explaining to him the basic rules for settling an argument with a friend, had listened to Jaime, but also provided the adult assistance he and his playmate needed. I did not pick up any negligence or overly permissive behavior or attitude on her part.

Kevin, at this point, said, "He's just a kid. All of these things that the teacher talks about are things kids grow out of. The situation is going to fix itself. I don't have a problem with him in terms of listening. When I mean business, he knows it, and he does what I tell him to. I think the teacher has got to learn how to be firm with him. I was the same way. He needs to know that the teachers are on to him, and he'll straighten out."

In the movie *Rashomon*, an incident occurs in the forest. Each of the four people involved tells a completely different version of what actually transpired. Every story depicts events contradicted by those in the other stories; the main characters in the four stories are identical, but the events wildly differ depending on who is telling the tale. Listening to Isabelle's and Kevin's responses to the teacher's complaints brought back the feeling of that film. Isabelle emerged shaken and overwrought as a result of what she considered to be a report of substantial difficulties that her son was experiencing at school. According to her, the situation was cause for careful planning and much soul-searching. She felt that Jaime was being singled out by his teacher and might learn to identify himself as a poor student. She was concerned about Jaime's self-esteem and the negative impact that these experiences might have on the development of his overall socialization and learning skills.

But according to Kevin there was little to talk about. "Whatever is going on will straighten itself out in due time."

If anything, he seemed mildly annoyed with the teacher for calling difficulties to his and Isabelle's attention. "These are the things kids do. And then they grow out of them and don't do them anymore." That Jaime might be experiencing difficulties with which he might need help, even professional assistance, was outside Kevin's purview.

Kevin had attended elementary school in Barbados. There, compared to New York City public schools, classroom procedures were formal and highly structured. Individualized attention, based on Kevin's description of his school masters, was provided in the form of corporal punishment to students who, for any reason, were not conforming to the teacher's expectations. Bajan ("Bajan" is the adjective form of the word "Barbados") custom dictated that parents left school business to the teachers and headmasters. For a Bajan parent or family member to complain about a teacher or a school situation was unusual and, except under rarest circumstance, considered to be poor form, a sign of incivility. Becoming involved collaboratively with school decisions and recommendations was something that made Kevin uncomfortable. He seemed to resist the very possibility that it might be necessary.

Creating a Team

Isabelle voiced disappointment in response to Kevin's position. "What happens is that I am left to deal with Jaime's school situation all by myself because, according to Kevin, there is nothing to worry about. His attitude is basically that Jaime is a great kid and that things will work out fine for him. I know that he doesn't think that Jaime needs any special help. Kevin thinks that because he got by without any help,

Jaime will, too. The thing is Jaime is not Kevin. Jaime *may* need more help than Kevin did, and we've got to find out if that's the situation."

When questioned how he felt about this, Kevin said that Isabelle was overreacting. I asked him whether he was aware of how she felt about the situation, and when he said yes, I requested that he summarize for Isabelle what he understood to be her experience with Jaime. Kevin did a good job of encapsulating Isabelle's concerns. He included the fact that she felt that what was going on in school might indicate that Jaime needed help that he, at present, was not receiving. Kevin also stated that she was feeling troubled by what was going on.

Isabelle agreed with Kevin's assessment of her feelings. I commended Kevin's listening skills and ability to articulate the gist of what Isabelle had been feeling—even though he did not feel the same way. I then asked him what plan of action he would suggest if he did share Isabelle's feelings. Although he was unsure what he would do, he supposed he would do something.

"Can you imagine feeling the way you know Isabelle feels—as you described her feelings—and doing nothing?" I said.

Kevin acknowledged that he would not feel good about doing that, but he did agree to the three of us figuring out an action plan that would include *both* his feelings and Isabelle's.

To which I said the following: "You are both in solid agreement that whatever Jaime needs should be arranged for him. You disagree not so much at this point about what he needs—because neither of you actually feels like you know what he needs—but you are disagreeing about how to go about confirming what he may need or not need in terms of help at school. You've got signals from his teacher that you, Isabelle, are feeling indicate a certain urgency in responding and which you, Kevin, feel may not be all that significant. Now, you are both experts on the subject of Jaime, the person, but I think it would make sense at this point to consult with someone who is an expert on students and their learning styles because that is the issue at hand. We have two working hypotheses that can be the focus of what you, as parents, would like to learn from a thorough evaluation of Jaime's learning style. In order to gain the kind of information that would help you both decide what kind of help, *if any*, Jaime needs as a student, the evaluator would have to help you figure out, for one, whether Jaime is the kind of student that Kevin was. Is he essentially doing fine but perhaps is somewhat distracted and overly playful at school? Maybe that's what the evaluation will show. Or is he having difficulties that he may not be able to articulate? Difficulties that he may need help with? Whatever we find out puts us ahead in our efforts to understand Jaime. Once we have more information, we can make a better-informed decision about how to interpret what his teacher is saying about him. With a clearer idea about what his learning problems are, we can also evaluate whether perhaps his personality is not meshing with his teacher's style. Maybe it's a poor teacher-student fit?"

Kevin responded, "Maybe. It could be a bad fit."

"Okay," I proceeded. "So how do you feel about having a learning specialist evaluate Jaime?"

We discussed the issue at length. Isabelle and Kevin agreed that it would take the pressure off them as parents to have more information about Jaime. It also might give them more objectivity in assessing and responding to his teacher's comments. Rather than debating each other on how to proceed, they were beginning to work together as a team for Jaime's—and their own—benefit. Rather than competing with each other in the area *between* them, they were building understandings; their middle ground was emerging.

Their individual views of the situation were no longer competing for dominance; who was right or wrong about what Jaime needed no longer would be their focus *because their goal was to act as allies and advocates for their son.*

I spoke to them about deemphasizing the idea that there had to be a right and a wrong person when they had a disagreement. "The idea of opening up the dialogue so that both of you develop a full appreciation of what the other is thinking and feeling is going to be much more valuable in the long run than deciding who is right or wrong or who is to blame or not to blame about a particular issue."

I told them I was impressed that they seemed united in seeking to learn more about how each could help Jaime. "Jaime, according to his teacher, needs to learn more about cooperation. Your coming together to work on his behalf as a team will teach him more about cooperation than any conversations on the subject."

Neither had been required to give up his or her beliefs. Neither had been told that his or her beliefs were right or wrong. Both were asked to hold onto what they thought and felt but to also be open to new information that *might* change their opinion about what was needed for their son.

As we prepared to leave the session, Kevin said, "Did you know that Barbados has the highest literacy rate in the Western Hemisphere?"

I said that I hadn't been aware of that. "I think somebody who comes from a place that knows how to educate its youngsters effectively is in a good position to make valuable contributions to the way things work here. Your positive experience and background is a valuable asset for the family."

I was trying to validate Kevin's pride in his country and simultaneously communicate a need for him to make an *active* comparison of the situation there and the current situation his son faced. I pointed out that what may have made sense and been expected in Barbados—that parents stand back and allow school administrators to do their job without much input or participation from parents—was not necessarily what would make sense in New York City.

Evaluation Results

Upon reading the results of the evaluation, both Isabelle and Kevin were surprised. Jaime reportedly had been identified as having a specific auditory processing deficit. Contrary to any indication that he was overly playful, it seemed that the evaluator felt he was trying very hard to make sense of what was required of him at school but that, in spite of his good effort and motivation—due to his auditory processing weakness—Jaime continued to get lost and feel frustrated.

Isabelle was relieved to find that the report had exonerated her parenting style as a factor in Jaime's school difficulties. Kevin now saw that his son was dealing with a problem with which he had never had to contend. Both parents felt that the information would help them move forward in getting Jaime the help he needed to succeed in school.

With this helpful information in hand, the couple faced a series of meetings with school personnel—social workers, education evaluators, psychologists, school administrators—which would use the evaluation results to craft an individualized education program for Jaime. There was talk of a small, self-contained class or possibly a team-teaching class—one conducted by the combined efforts of a general education and special education teacher. A third alternative: Jaime could remain in general education, and the services he needed could be delivered as part of his general education program. How would the couple decide which setting would work best for Jaime? Should they simply leave the decision up to the school professionals? They were given a week to think over the alternatives and then return to a follow-up meeting.

As before Jaime's evaluation, each parent had a differing perspective on how to respond to the school and decide what would work best for Jaime. Isabelle distrusted having Jaime separated from a general education classroom, afraid that he would feel stigmatized. Kevin felt that the school professionals probably knew what was best for his son, and he was reluctant to question or challenge whatever they might suggest. How could the parents make a decision that respected both their opinions and perspectives?

Again, I urged them to broaden their knowledge base and see if that helped ease the decision-making pressure. Since they had a good feeling about the woman who had evaluated Jaime, I suggested they consult with her if possible. I also gave them the names of three well-known, not-for-profit parent-support agencies whom they could contact for advice and support. Once again, instead of arguing about their different perspectives, they were able to work together for their son's benefit; the middle ground strengthened.

SECTION 2: BEYOND HELP WITH JAIME

Their dealings with the public school and special education system were never easy, but they began to feel less perilous. For one thing, going into meetings, each felt an alliance with the other. Kevin got positive feedback concerning his participation in these meetings from Isabelle and the school personnel themselves. Isabelle reported that Kevin spoke convincingly about his son's strengths and cooperativeness at home, while also underscoring points made in the evaluation that clarified that Jaime, to achieve his potential at school, needed—more than criticisms of his behavior—structured help to overcome the specific auditory deficit that the evaluator had identified. Different cultures feature varying, sometimes contradictory, models for how strong men act. Which is more important, the externalized behavior or the trait—for example, strength of character—that the behavior is presumed to represent? Kevin learned to demonstrate the strength of his presence differently here than he had in Barbados.

Isabelle reported, "Jaime is still a handful. I'm feeling that Kevin and I worked well to help him, but we still have trouble helping ourselves. There is a lot of tension between us. We argue about a lot of things—too many things and too much of the time. Sometimes I find myself in an argument with Kevin, and I'm not even sure what it's about or why it's happening. It just seems to be a way that we are together. It wasn't always like this, and I know that it bothers me a lot. Doesn't it bother you, Kevin?"

Kevin nodded without saying anything. His eyes seemed pinned momentarily to a spot on the floor. Perhaps he was remembering something.

"You said that you've been arguing a lot, but that it wasn't always like this," I said. "How would you feel about taking turns and telling me about when things were different and, if you can, give me your ideas on when the arguing started, when the mood of the relationship began to change."

The Path to Parenthood

Isabelle began, followed by Kevin. Occasionally, they interjected comments or information to flesh out each other's memories of how their relationship developed. What follows is a summary of their recounting.

They met at a mutual friend's Fourth of July barbecue. Isabelle had arrived late. The hostess of the party introduced them, and they began speaking and remained together for the rest of the evening. They talked and laughed and danced, and although they went home separately that night, by the end of the week, they were separating only when one or the other or both had to go to work. He was twenty-eight and she was twenty-six. Almost a year to the day after meeting, they married.

The first phase of their relationship—the "honeymoon" period—brought each into a close-up view of each other. Their two worlds melded with the heat of erotic infatuation. They referred to each other as "soul mates."

The first three years of their married life were, in many ways, something of an extended holiday. There were conflicts but nothing that cut deeply enough to disturb their sense of connection. They left the city together frequently. They would cook together, and each would cook for the other separately. They talked playfully, shared dreams and concerns late into the night. Whatever it was that they were doing with their lives during this time, however they defined it, they shared a sense that they were doing it together.

Each worked at jobs that were acceptable but not particularly exciting. Neither had yet made a serious career decision, but they were making enough money to live comfortably. He was a salaried computer technician and she the administrative assistant in a busy law office. During her free time, she designed jewelry, sometimes sketched, and loved to read. Kevin filled the house with acoustic guitar playing and singing, which Isabelle enjoyed.

Their life as two married people without children proceeded. This prolonged honeymoon wave had moved across the ocean of their time together with grace and even a touch of majesty. They came to rely on the honeymoon spirit as if it were a fixture on their horizon—as durable and reliable as the bridge they could glimpse from their living room window. If that wave were to crash, consequences would be serious, and so they were when it did.

From the day that Isabelle found out she was pregnant, things began to shift. Before, their varying spending styles had been evident. What was the difference if they went a few hundred over budget if, in the end, they could always cover the unexpected? Not enough to raise as an issue demanding attention. But now their budget couldn't cover overages in the same way. To accommodate the expenses involved in raising a baby, they were going to have to be disciplined if their money was going to stretch to cover costs. And even then they would have to find ways to compensate for Isabelle working less, as they were planning she would. Economizing brought home the reality of living in a much less carefree phase than before.

Prior to this time, Isabelle, much the thriftier, had always accepted or made light of Kevin's tendency to spend more freely; she now felt forced into trying to monitor and/or restrict him. New tensions and conflicts were felt by both partners.

Isabelle wished Kevin to be neater and cleaner around the house. She wanted more help with shopping and laundering—large categorical changes that she first requested and then demanded. He wanted her to be interested in having sex more frequently and less interested in neatness, cleaning, spending, shopping, and laundering. He also wanted her to talk about changes in the relationship without creating the feeling in him that she saw him as responsible for most, if not all, of what needed to be improved in their life together. From her greatest supporter, he felt she had become his greatest critic.

Smaller issues—like whether the toilet seat cover should be left up or down—were once considered worth mentioning but not worth getting upset about. She had, in the past, asked him , "Please put the toilet seat cover down after you use it." To which he responded, "Okay, but can you leave it up after you use it?" Now, Isabelle came back with,

"If we can't cooperate about something like this, what are we going to do when the baby gets here?"

Kevin had associated a feeling of largesse with their being together. In Isabelle's presence, he'd felt that, seen through her eyes, he was perfect; he felt adored. He could recall thinking soberly that she would not want him to be different than the way he was, and she had told him so. In tandem with that, he believed that she felt the same way when in his presence. On this basis of perfect attunement they pillared their claim to being soul mates. Because he now felt that he was viewed as highly imperfect, and that they were quite imperfectly attuned, this very painful question occurred to him: were they still soul mates? And it was painful not only because it occurred to him but also because he realized that it might also occur to her. And what would that mean? Could they—as a couple—survive with the spell broken?

Jaime's birth brought a flood of loving and triumphant feelings for Isabelle and Kevin to share. Both parents adored their lively and beautiful son.

Kevin responded to the need for more income by working overtime and taking on freelance work. Isabelle was on extended maternity leave and did not intend to return to work full time for an undetermined period, perhaps six months or more. She appreciated what Kevin was doing—the family needed the money—but he was around less and was more tired when he was around. She yearned for the kind of intimate connection they had once shared.

Having a child drew the couple closer. Raising the baby was more an effort of noninterference—on Kevin's part—than cooperation. Isabelle and Kevin did not see eye-to-eye on certain child-rearing ideas, but Kevin gave ground graciously to the mother of his child. Essentially, where they differed they called a truce. Negotiating their differences, hearing each other out and resolving conflicts between themselves was a goal that they had not yet accomplished.

Extending the Middle Ground

We worked with three basic communication exercises discussed at length elsewhere in this book—"the Basic Three-Step Exercise," "Reaching Out from the Inside," and "One Talks, the Other Doesn't"—so that Isabelle and Kevin could experience a conversation in which they took turns, in which they expressed themselves fully without making accusations or implying blame, and in which the listener explicitly acknowledged the speaker's feelings. The emphasis was on listening to and validating each other's feelings.

This is one issue we worked on in depth using the exercises: Isabelle had asked for more help in feeding and cleaning Jaime. When Kevin attempted to provide that help, she hovered over him and Jaime, and she made supervisory and sometimes disparaging comments. If he deviated from her method of performing a particular task, she would stridently comment, "No, not that way," and take over the activity. The pattern of Isabelle's reluctance to relinquish control of Jaime's care, even now when Kevin had clear command of Jaime when they were together, still affected the way the parents interacted at times. Kevin had felt minimized and unappreciated by what she had done.

Isabelle acknowledged that she had put Kevin in a bad position where his feelings were not being taken into account. She further stated that she understood that he probably felt unappreciated for doing—taking care of Jaime—what she had said she would appreciate him doing. She apologized and added, "Kevin has never hurt or endangered Jaime. The way I handled things might have been appropriate if he had actually mishandled Jaime, but he never has done this. That's why I believe I do owe you an apology."

Kevin, hearing this apology, seemed to come out from behind a cloud. He said that he hadn't really thought out anything she'd said, but it all made sense to him; without even realizing it, he had been angry about some things, and this was part of them. With a meek smile, he said he accepted the apology, almost as if he had been given a present and was embarrassed at the tenderness of the thought behind it.

Food for thought: The myth of the "soul mate" in which Isabelle and Kevin were so heavily invested, for many couples, militates against acknowledging that differences— even between persons who love each other dearly—are inevitable. If people want to hang onto the term "soul mate" and keep it within bounds of human possibility, they've got to bring it down to earth sufficiently to acknowledge that "rightness of fit"—no matter how right— *always* includes some differences. Otherwise, the phrase is an exercise in sadomasochistic perfectionism that ultimately weakens and destroys the bond it purportedly exults.

Our focus on Isabelle and Kevin's communication intensified the couple's own awareness of ways to retrace the steps that had led to their feeling so disconnected. They had become inured to noticing that virtually *all* the tender considerations and special planning within their relationship had become directly connected to or focused on Jaime.

They had gotten into the habit of ignoring each other. We discussed the idea that they needed to plan fun times for themselves, as a couple, if they were going to supplant the mood of disconnection that had taken over their partnership—romantic times, quiet times for themselves to feel the unity of their own presence in their own lives, not simply as adjuncts to their son's development. This was the challenge presented to them in our work at this phase.

In his perceptive and highly recommended book, *All You Need Is Love and Other Lies about Marriage*, John W. Jacobs writes about what he calls a "myth"—that children solidify family life. He contrasts this to what he believes is the underlying reality—that children can threaten their parents' relationship. The threat, as he describes it, has to do with children appropriating the lion's share of each partner's concerns and physical and emotional stamina, as well as leaving too little adult attention to be shared between parents as lovers, companions, and friends—the very situation that Isabelle and Kevin found themselves in.

If parents with a solid relationship are able to continue giving each other *at least some* of the attention that they each need, the children will be become prime beneficiaries of the parents' efforts to keep their love alive. Without this effort, the children, no matter how attentively cared for, miss out on growing up with an atmosphere of love and caring *around* them.

The World-Within-the-World

A noted family therapist, Ron Taffel spoke to me about a couple he met while conducting a study on good marriages. This couple enjoyed a long and happy relationship in which they, for many years running, made it a point, on an average of four nights a week, to take a twenty-minute walk together at nearly the same time in the evening. A sense of peace accompanied them on these wanderings. Whereas an emotional home base can be an anxious place for many, a home base within the middle ground often fosters a sense of inner peace.

I spoke to Isabelle and Kevin about the possibility of creating some rituals that would give them a sense of their identity as a couple. We brainstormed to devise things that they could regularly do together that they would enjoy or, at least, that they would think were worth trying and seeing if they might develop into a steady activity to look forward to. Although they couldn't come up with something that they could plan on doing four or more times a week, they did think of a number of ideas that they could do one time or more each month that, put together, amounted to a series of events that they could look forward to and identify as *their* time together. They would try to get to a movie at least once a month. They would go for a drive, get out of the city at least for a few hours once every other week if not more frequently. Fortunately, they enjoyed similar reading material—both liked mysteries and fiction generally—and they both enjoyed reading to each other and being read to; they would see if they could have a book that they could follow and relax with together a few times a week. The list went on and on. Rather than compiling lists of complaints, they focused on lists of possibilities for making things better. The mood between them improved.

And what of their lives together as lovers? They had gotten to the point that angers and resentments had crept into their way of being together and blocked erotic feelings on both sides. Neither was satisfied with what had been going on at any level.

Interestingly, the week after our first foray into the quality of the sensual encounters between them—directly sexual and not—Kevin came in with something he wanted to share with me and Isabelle. He was a songwriter as well as a guitarist and singer and had awakened in the middle of the night to dash down some lines. He said, "They may be lyrics to a song. I'm not sure. I think maybe they are just the lines of a poem. In any case, this is how it goes." With his permission, I include it here:

On the corner of tomorrow

On the corner
of tomorrow
in my dream

I smile at you
And you smile at me
as you did then
I see your smile
And you see mine

I long to meet you there
meet you, *there*.
meet *you*—there
meet you there
on the corner of tomorrow

Meet Me There

Kevin's poem became a motif that we revisited on various occasions. *He longed to see her looking at him as she did then*, to meet her while looking and feeling *that way* himself and for her to understand that this was what he dreamed of. They still were within each other's dreams. They could still, if the term "soul mate" can be reconfigured to a use that benefits humans, be soul mates. He was affirming that things may have changed, and we can't meet in the past, but we can transport some of the allure of what we know we've had into the moment we are living in and the ones we will encounter. Kevin had created an image that he and Isabelle could come alive within. He had helped create a beautiful space within their burgeoning middle ground. By joining him within the imagery, by responding to the feeling, by reciprocating the excitement, she made the moment real.

EXERCISE: TEAMWORK QUIZ

On a separate sheet of paper, answer "T" for "true" or "F" for "false" to each question. Then, have your partner do the same.

____ When the welfare of our child(ren) is the issue, my partner and I do a good job of cooperating.

____ I feel appreciated for the time and effort I put in with my child(ren).

____ I appreciate that my partner is doing as good a job as possible in fulfilling parental responsibilities.

____ We keep track together of what must be done for our child(ren).

____ I can rely on my partner's support to help me think through how to approach important problems or projects involving the child(ren).

____ Although we may disagree on some details of how to handle our parenting responsibilities, there is a great deal of mutual respect in how we function as parents.

____ If I had to say whether my partner and I were compatible specifically in terms of our parenting styles, I would say yes.

____ My partner has helped me feel good about the job I do as a parent.

____ I help my partner feel good about the job he or she is doing as a parent.

____ There are always new things to learn when you are a parent. My partner and I each play an active role in keeping up with the need to be well informed on parenting issues.

Scoring Procedure

For each T, count 1 point. For each F, count no points. A score of 0 to 2 indicates that there is much to accomplish before you and your partner will feel that you are an effective parenting team. A score of 3 to 7 indicates that you have some of the basics of teamwork but need to keep working at it. Minor improvements in your cooperation around parenting will result in major benefit for all family members—including, of course, your child(ren). A score of 7 or above indicates an impressive level of cooperation and teamwork is already in place in your relationship.

EXERCISE: KEEPING LOVE ALIVE

On a separate sheet of paper, answer "T" for "true" or "F" for "false" to each question. Then, have your partner do the same.

____ Even though our schedules are hectic, my partner and I manage to spend quality time together at least a few times a week.

____ Over the last six weeks, my partner and I have had two evenings to ourselves.

____ Over the past six months, my partner and I have gone out together—without any children—at least six times.

____ I regularly approach my partner and make some kind of romantic gesture.

____ My partner regularly approaches me in a way that I understand and appreciate as romantic.

____ I do not feel that my partner takes my love for granted.

____ I do not take my partner's love for granted.

____ My partner and I have established our own loving rituals that we look forward to experiencing together.

____ Taking into account the year immediately prior to today, I feel satisfied with the sex life that my partner and I share.

____ Taking into account the year immediately prior to today, I feel satisfied with the level of affection shared in our relationship.

Scoring Procedure

For each T, count 1 point. For each F, count no points. Scores of 0–3 indicate that you and your partner are in dire need of spending more time together and improving the romantic dimension of your relationship. Scores of 4 to 9 indicate that you have a lot of strengths in your relationship but need to actively communicate about areas of dissatisfaction so that problem areas are addressed. Scores of 9 or 10 indicate that your relationship has great strengths and satisfactions for you to keep enjoying.

Chapter 6

SYNCOPATED RHYTHMS

NOTE

Out of the whole book, the next few pages—the section called Part One—are the most dense. The rhythm of communication—which can include the request for a change from your partner *and* his or her response—often involves dynamics that are challenging, both to live with and understand. In Part One, I introduce an idea that I am confident will help you understand why certain requests for change take longer and are more difficult than it may seem they need to be. I introduce the idea with an illustration drawn from the work of a brilliant British psychoanalyst and his experiment involving how babies respond to the introduction of something new—a change—presented to them. Please stay with me, and I promise you'll find this discussion useful.

PART 1

Coming together and sliding apart define the rhythms of partnership. And these rhythms vary widely from couple to couple. Some pairs execute their dance with elegance and flair, coordinating matched half-turns, quick stops, even pirouettes with grace. Others, in sharp contrast, move along with an awkward jumble of miscues, missteps, and missed opportunities.

As partners advance through the life cycle, their *awareness* of the meaning, purpose, and direction of the steps that each takes becomes heightened. Partners ask, "Where are we now?"—in this new phase of our relationship—but more emphatically, "Why have we moved to where we are? What does it mean in terms of 'us'? In terms of me?"

We ask whether our partner's sense of what they are doing has escaped us or whether they've missed their own marks. Have they turned away from possibilities for mutuality? At times, we may ask ourselves the same.

Baby as Teacher—A Brief Digression

D. W. Winnicott, a British pediatrician-psychoanalyst, is acknowledged as a major influence on the work and thought of such baby experts as Doctors Benjamin Spock and Terry Brazelton. He hosted a radio show on the BBC, lectured widely, and wrote extensively. He developed groundbreaking theories on the psychology of human development. I'd like to focus on an experiment with infants that Winnicott conducted; it was designed to explore the meaning of the infant's various responses to new objects in the environment—ones that posed *demands* on their attention, to be more specific. Under what circumstances do infants respond well to the new objects and under what conditions do they avoid noticing or responding to the new demands placed on them? These were the questions Winnicott wished this research to address.

At first, Winnicott places a shiny surgical spatula in his consulting room where an infant can see it. Once the infant moves toward the shiny object, she invariably becomes involved in an intense round of play with it. The baby bites, sucks, waves, and "feeds" the spatula to her mother and tosses and retrieves it.

For the sake of comparison, Winnicott—on a separate occasion—does not allow the infant to discover the spatula but presents it immediately to the infant as she is carried into the consulting room. When she cannot discover the spatula for herself, the infant consistently lays it aside, shows no interest in it, or protests against involvement with the glistening tool.

Winnicott concludes that, in presenting the spatula directly to the infant rather than giving her a chance to discover it for herself, the infant had been deprived of an opportunity to connect the spatula in the consulting room with an internal event. This "event" is a subjective phenomenon through which the infant learns to associate the spatula with what she is experiencing internally—I call this the infant's "inner splash" of discovery. So picture, as the infant reaches out to touch the spatula, there is a simultaneous inner event that acquaints her with her awareness of the event transpiring in the room.

This process defines how the infant's experience of what is outside her becomes known and validated for her internally as "real." The inner splash is what binds the infant's awareness of what is outside to an *inner process*. The experience serves the dual function of making what is inside *and* what is outside her feel real. That these events are conjoined in her experience becomes a hallmark for her experience of what is real. It is part of what the infant must experience and bring to awareness in order to learn to clearly distinguish between what goes on inside and outside her and the relationship between the two types of experience.

> **Key point:** The infant generates the process of getting to know an external object from the inside out. The infant learns to "take in" new experience, while, simultaneously, an internalized awareness of herself as alive and responsive in connection with her surroundings becomes stimulated, strengthened, and developed. This explains how the infant's learning about her environment is inextricable from her learning about herself.

When Winnicott places the spatula in his room and allows the infant time to find it, as he did initially, he calls this space of time—between the infant's being exposed to the new object and the infant's taking it up as an object of play—a "period of hesitation." The infant needs this to coordinate inside learning with learning about external reality, in order to make her involvement with the new experience truly her own.

The period of hesitation embodies within it a moment of ambivalence toward whether to act in relation to a new opportunity for play or learning; the period of hesitation provides a momentary platform upon which the infant can exercise a choice, to respond or not.

Impingement

Winnicott believed that the reason the child does not develop interest in the spatula when it is presented too directly is that the spatula, under those conditions, is experienced as *separating* the infant from her internal process of discovery. Separated from the splash of discovery, the infant does not take action as a result of an internal signal. The infant, in responding to the object that has been thrust upon her, is no longer mediating the environment from within but is reacting to an intrusion on her *inner* space by the environment. Winnicott termed this intrusion an "impingement."

He felt that infants were naturally resilient but that too many experiences of this type put the infant at risk for underdevelopment of a deep and necessary connection to herself in relation to her exploration of the environment *and* of her inner identity.

The infant who is too often impinged upon comes to identify with being overwhelmed by her environment. She defines herself in a way that reflects her being pushed around by her circumstances without being able to effectively push back; if integrated into her core identity, this leads to passivity and depression.

To avoid the experience of impingement, the infant will sometimes, as Winnicott discovered, disengage interest in the spatula, or any new thing in the environment that is thrust too directly on her. This is an important self-preservative measure.

The Lost and Then Found Rhythm

Learning is, of course, no simple operation. Think about the pattern a new infant, Emily, follows. She, as we can predict, rejects the spatula when it is imposed on her; she protests against involvement. However, *following* a period of hesitation, she *then* turns her attention to it.

Emily rejects the spatula at first because it impinged upon her, but after a time she *finds* it (on her own terms) and claims it. Having discovered it for herself, she rejoices. She takes it in and plays with it—biting, sucking, waving, as infants do. She makes it her own. In this way, her *sense* of initiative, like a sixth sense, develops.

She had "lost" the spatula—because it was presented in a way that was unacceptable to her—and through the act of *losing* it, she *preserves* the possibility of *finding* it and making it her own.

Do not be misled by the metaphor in use—talking about a baby and expecting you to find it relevant to your problems with your partner. I am most assuredly *not* assuming that this person in your life is drooling and crawling around on the rug. Still, we can learn something about ourselves from thinking about this elemental model of how adjustment to new things and changes in our environment affect a tiny human.

PART 2

How Do We Ask a Partner to Make a Change?

Winnicott's study is relevant to us because it outlines conditions needed for tiny humans to adjust to what is new in their surroundings. We can learn a few valuable lessons from this study to help us approach our partners when we wish *them* to adjust to something new. It can help us, ourselves, when we are asked to make changes.

Most importantly, these ideas can help us understand our partners' reactions to our requests for changes that will, in all probability, often be disappointingly slow in coming.

The infant, when experiencing the "something new" as an impingement, simply ignores or rejects the new thing. She does not accept the terms and conditions under which it is being offered and will not acknowledge that the issue has been presented. Often, the "something new" must be lost so that it can be later found.

Joyce and Ray

If our partners feel cornered, impinged upon, will we get a genuine and considered response to the issue we would like to discuss? More than likely their response will reflect how they feel about being coerced into responding; the issue will likely get completely lost. And, at this point, it may become more difficult to reopen.

First example: Joyce wants to talk to Ray about planning more time together on the weekends. She anticipates he will be resistant and that this will cause her to become angry. By the time she decides to speak to him about it, she is angry about the resistance that she anticipates and starts the conversation by yelling and criticizing. Rather than deal with the issue that she wanted to speak about, Ray's response centers exclusively on how unfair it feels for her to approach him this way. Nothing useful is accomplished, and the couple is further away from the middle ground. Ray had no opportunity for a period of hesitation.

Now let's think about a way Joyce might have incorporated a period of hesitation for him into her approach. Joyce realizes that she is anticipating Ray will be resistant and that, if he is, she will get angry. When they are together, she prefaces her approach with, "I've been thinking about this for a while, and when I think about it, I start feeling like you will put me off if I bring up the subject of planning time together over the weekend. I then begin to get angry thinking about it and feel like if I don't do something to short-circuit my mood, I'm going to have a hard time talking to you. Does that make sense to you?"

Rather than yelling or criticizing Ray for something he hasn't even done yet, her statement and question give him a heads-up: to her, the issue is important. The clear implication of what she says is that she wants to avoid a fight *and* that she is having trouble bringing up this issue. She invites Ray to look at the issue with her. Her question is not aggressive but requires that he take in her experience before he responds.

As far as dealing with her target issue—making plans over the weekend—she does not put him on the hot seat but lets him improvise a way to approach the issue on his terms. Also, he is not given an ultimatum about how he can respond. She conveys valuable information—her sensitivity to feeling that he may put her off—to him. Compared with the previous example, this approach makes a middle-ground response from Ray more possible.

In the first example, Joyce offers no period of hesitation, and the results are not good. In the second, she offers room for him to hesitate if he needs to. The results of the second example are promising. There is a good chance that Ray will respond well, and they will have their discussion and make plans for getting together on the weekends—the outcome that Joyce is looking for. So that would be fine.

However, what if Ray doesn't respond well to the second approach? Let's discuss a third situation that can be trying but often works well in the end. Ray is in no mood to talk about what Joyce wants to talk about, and it doesn't matter much whether she presents it as she did in example one or two. It's the wrong time for her to bring up the issue, but there's no way she can know that because there are no clear signs that anything is wrong. In fact, there may not be anything wrong; it may simply be that Ray is preoccupied. Let's say he has got to make an important decision about work—maybe accepting an offer from his boss, assuming a major change in his job responsibilities, or moving to a new department, which he had not considered at all until this time. Joyce approaches him and he puts her off. What are her options? What makes sense for her to do at this point?

It is important for her to have some understanding of Ray's unavailability. If this is the first time she has tried to bring up the issue, she can ask if there is another time that they can discuss it. If Ray can't pick one, she can ask him to bring it up in the near future when he feels ready to. In that way, she directly provides a period of hesitation for him.

He may bring it up shortly, and the issue may get addressed quickly. Let's assume it doesn't happen that way. Let's assume she waits for him to initiate a conversation, to express interest in what she wanted to talk to him about. She waits a day and then reapproaches him. At this point, he still feels preoccupied and puts her off again. She is disappointed and lets him know it. Okay. She hasn't criticized him at this point. By raising the issue again, she rather gently tendered him another heads-up, another point of emphasis that establishes further credibility for the issue as important. She is asserting herself but not coercing him or even curtailing his period of hesitation. This patience is sometimes necessary in relationships.

Now, let's change the scenario. Let's say that Ray has no job change to think about, that he's stalling simply because he'd like to avoid dealing with Joyce's issue. He senses that the discussion will be difficult for him. Given that Joyce has approached him twice and he has not responded, he *may* at this point have had an opportunity to get used to the idea that this is something he will have to face and, thinking about it that way, may prepare himself to talk about it. If so, this is an example of a communication process that has been worked through to a point where a difficult issue begins to be addressed. Sounds like pulling teeth? Sounds slow? It can be. Working on a relationship involves this kind of work at times.

Again, a lot of people question what the "work" in "couples' work" means. The series of interactions that Joyce and Ray went through—having the patience and perseverance and remaining open to feeling out what needs to be done to get a stalled dialogue moving—those qualities all figure into the work in couples' work on communication.

Joyce didn't blow up at Ray during the first two approaches, *and* she didn't abandon the issue that she needed to have addressed. That took work. And Ray—although I was starting to have my doubts about him—was able to compose himself after trying to avoid the issue at hand, and he finally *found* it, the lost and found rhythm, for himself. He made use of the periods of hesitation extended to him.

In the end, they both came through for each other. This is what is meant by the middle ground. It was on both of their terms. And it corresponded, in its idiosyncratic way, to both of their rhythms. Easy going? Not really. Impossibly difficult? Not for Joyce and Ray. For you? Probably not. You never know unless you try.

If you do the hard work and still do not get any satisfaction, consider going through the process with a third person, a therapist, to add additional gravity to what is at stake in these simple requests for dialogue and for finding the time to plan together—the quality and, ultimately, the vitality of your relationship.

More on Rhythm

The odd accents and inconsistent measures that make up the rhythm of communication result from the unevenness of our histories. Unresolved feelings, moods, associations, varying temperaments, periods of hesitation—all take up space within the communication process and place us in relation to each other in ways that are idiosyncratic, difficult to anticipate. The most common rhythms of communication involve syncopation.

If you made a statement, and your partner simply gave you a cooperative response right off the bat, wouldn't it be wonderful? Sure. But the gaps exist for reasons that need to be worked with and through.

Reasons sometimes can be used inappropriately, but there is a legitimate need for most of us to maintain a style of response that includes irregularity, especially periods of hesitation. These periods of hesitation often appear to be indistinguishable from stonewalling or rejecting one's partner. Being able to read the difference between the two can improve your communication process markedly. Important work gets done during that period of hesitation. With an infant, the use of this period connects directly to identity development.

For adults, when a period of hesitation is needed but not provided or tolerated, the partner who is approached cannot respond authentically but can only rebel or comply. This does not mean that your partner has to wait for the inspiration of feeling that she is absolutely right before she can discuss the possibility of screwing the cap back on the toothpaste. What it means is that if no period (or periods) of hesitation are offered, the power struggle can take on the character of the unstoppable force colliding with the immovable object. Not usually a productive meeting.

The goal is to be able to discuss expectations, become aware of our partner's position on any given issue, and the feelings and thoughts supporting this position. We need to expose our position and the feelings and thoughts that underlie it as well and then negotiate something pragmatic and flexible enough to work for both.

If you are asking your partner to change something, or if you are being asked to make a change, do either of you adjust responses to accommodate (or anticipate) a need for a period of hesitation as a part of the rhythm of response? If not, think about trying this and seeing if this can work for you.

> **Tip:** The harder the pursuer of an issue pursues, the more that issue becomes registered to the pursuer, and the more difficult it becomes for the other partner to integrate it as her issue and take ownership for her part in the problem.

The period of hesitation is a space in which the dialogue breathes. Without the breathing space, the issue has no means for regulating pace unless time-outs are devised, as recommended in chapter 7. The time-outs, for all intents and purposes, serve the same function as periods of hesitation.

> **FAQ #1:** Does this mean that once you've presented an idea to your partner, you need to muzzle yourself and not bring it up unless he does?

ANSWER: No. As you saw with Joyce and Ray, although your rhythm of approach needs to be respectful of your partner's response pattern, you cannot depend on your significant other's rhythm to the extent that you ignore your own and feel shut down. Bring up the issue but try to do it in the form of an invitation. For example, Joyce says, "I realize you may not have had a chance to think about what we talked about earlier. Can we arrange a time that you think you'd be available to do that?" This gives Ray a chance to regain initiative in choosing the time. Or if the issue is even more delicate, "When do you think would be a good time to revisit this conversation we had about the weekend? You don't have to let me know right now, but if you can let me know within the next [whatever length of time seems reasonable], that would be great. Can you do that?" Inviting your partner to resume dialogue will tend to cut through resistance and, in some instances, help develop momentum in approaching difficult conversations.

FAQ #2: Aren't there some issues or situations—like verbal or physical abuse, for example—in which zero tolerance is appropriate and considering your partner's need for a "period of hesitation" is self-destructive?

ANSWER: Yes, absolutely. Abusive situations of any sort must be handled swiftly, and a self-focus—doing what is needed to preserve yourself—must be conscientiously maintained. Crises need to be handled with an emphasis on resolving the issue at hand immediately if possible and, if not, as soon as is possible. The period of hesitation is useful in understanding the patterns of communication in everyday living, not in emergency or abusive situations.

Is This Information Practical?

Being able to incorporate periods of hesitation into your dialogue rests on developing other skills such as containing or tolerating—within yourself and/or within your partner—anger and anxiety. Developing those skills is not easy. These are primary therapeutic goals. Couples' work is not easy. Create a middle ground and you've achieved something. It opens the door for many understandings and makes many techniques and insights—like these "period of hesitation" ideas—usable.

Engaging in couples' work without these skills is, as I say elsewhere about not having a middle ground, like trekking through the desert with a hole in your canteen. Knowing how powerful the results can be if you patch that hole can motivate you to do it!

When you consider this metaphor, think of the desert as the obstacle that the relationship faces when it is very troubled; the desert is not the relationship itself. The relationship includes areas outside its arid trouble zone; the middle ground is one. At least we hold out hope and work with this possibility—unless we decide that the relationship is over.

It may not be easy to patch the canteen given the circumstances, but the urgency of making this priority repair is underscored dramatically because of the heightened awareness of what is at stake: the survival of the relationship, finding a way out of the desert.

Sean listened patiently as I spoke with him about this idea of a period of hesitation. He then said, "I understand what you're saying. It sounds fine. In fact, it sounds like it would improve things between me and Julia. The thing is, I don't think we can do something like that. We're too angry. It takes something that we don't have. And it makes me feel worse hearing about it because we're not going to be able to use it. It just makes me all the more frustrated."

I paused for a moment. I had an impulse to defend my ideas but, at the same time, realized that what Sean said pointed precisely to where my work with him and his partner needed to go. I thanked him for his statement. I acknowledged that in order to develop a sensitivity to the rhythm of dialogue—to nurture appropriate pauses, times for integration of the other's point of view—a dimension of calm and reflection must either exist in the relationship or have potential to come into the relationship. Sean was saying that such a potential did not exist between himself and Julia. So what could he do with all this information?

To patch the hole and get to a point where other techniques can come into play, we needed to address essential skills like the ability to control the expression of anger and tolerate the anxiety of changes. Sean honestly felt that he and Julia couldn't do that, so we got to work on addressing this. They could work on the exercises if they hadn't or try them again if they had. They could be more diligent in analyzing the triggers that cause them to lose control in angry situations; that would be key to preventing destructive outbursts. Sean was saying that, even with heightened awareness, he could not feel any shred of optimism.

Sean's perspective gives our work a strong focus, not a point of termination.

Optimism versus Pessimism

Probably the greatest deterrent to taking a first step in the "new direction"—a positive change direction—is the feeling that taking that step will be meaningless because there is nothing beyond it.

Think of this: Two couples are both stuck in the desert. One is told that there is water within ten miles—an arduous but possible distance for them to travel. The other couple is told that the nearest water is four hundred miles away—a death sentence. Which of the two couples do you think will travel farther?

Research (see, for example, Susan Vaughan's *The Talking Cure*) indicates that holding a mental image of something hopeful as achievable increases possibilities for going further. Pessimism itself is debilitating, rendering your defenses against stress and panic significantly weakened; these conditions exacerbate whatever vulnerabilities already exist in the relationship.

Concepts like the period of hesitation expose possibilities for hope to the person who feels stuck. The issue for Sean is that he's pessimistic about whether he can learn to control his anger, deal with Julia's anger, or develop the patience needed to move forward. It's not that the period of hesitation concept doesn't benefit him; it's that it doesn't benefit him yet.

Sean faces hard challenges. But they're not harder than living in the hell of constant argument and disappointment. Because you have some good ideas that can be used as tools to help you take steps in your relationship, I realize, does not guarantee that they will work for you. You've got to work with them to make them work for you. It also helps to have them in the ready when you are in a position to use them.

Sean was saying, among other things, that he couldn't imagine things working out better. I answered, "You can't do that now. You can't imagine things working out better. Okay, I know that. But I can help you work on imagining being able to see a better day. And if you can imagine it, you will be a step closer to being able to do it. You have nothing to lose in trying to take this step." As actor Harvey Fierstein reputedly said in regard to suicide: "It's not one of those things you have to do now or you lose your chance. I mean, you can always do it later."

Before Throwing in the Towel

If you feel you cannot try to make a move, then I think it would have been impossible for you pick up this book. If you're looking for answers, you can find a way to imagine yourself taking positive steps. Feeling that you can't is a phase in the process that must be tolerated and worked with. It's possible that you will find that you cannot work things out with your partner. That is an existential possibility. If you make an all-out effort to repair the relationship, you will greatly benefit in future relationships, even if it turns out that you cannot go forward together. And then again, you never know until you try. You have nothing to lose by giving it everything you can. Trusting that—pragmatically—if you truly feel it is over, you can give yourself permission to leave. Pragmatically, the relationship has a life of its own, but it is not the same as your life. You can survive if the relationship does not. Being clear on this point will help you do everything that you *reasonably* can to heal your relationship.

Again, the middle ground is not about accomplishing the impossible. It's about developing a profound respect for, and sensitivity to, the possible.

Glass Half Filled?

Let's say that the glass—whether half filled or half empty, depending on who is reporting—represents diametrically opposite positions that partners sometimes assume when arguing. Is it unusual for two people to witness the same set of information and come to opposite conclusions about what the facts mean? Not at all, and this doesn't have to be a problem for couples if they can—as the old saw goes—discuss their way to resolution or agree to disagree and move on.

Problems develop for couples when one insists that his interpretation is the *only* one that makes sense. As discussed earlier, upon receiving a note from his teacher, Jaime's father felt it would be best to ignore it, act as if it were never received. At the same time, Jaime's mother felt a need to set up a meeting with the teacher as soon as possible. Breaking the stalemate came from adding new information, which generated a new perspective, recontextualizing the debate.

Whether the differing points of view result from a cursory look at hand or an obsessively thorough inspection can, in many situations, matter little. What matters is how partners approach negotiating their differences. How inclusive they are of each other's feelings on the subject is what makes the critical difference. Because they see things in a certain way, does it mean they relinquish any curiosity about their partner's viewpoint?

If either partner hunkers down in a non-negotiable stance, possibilities for a middle-ground conversation power down. Where a partner says or implies, "If you hear me, you'll agree with me; if you don't agree, it's because you are not listening," mutuality has been known to fly out the window so fast that, in some cases, it reportedly shatters the pane. Diametrically opposite views held stubbornly and self-righteously serve as the fulcrum on which many couples' power struggle teeters endlessly.

Reframing the issue can provide the needed breakthrough. Shift focus to a different aspect of the half-filled/half-empty glass. One partner may be in despair over the "half-empty" status of their relationship, thinking, "All that emptiness represents problems we have yet to solve." In this case, the counterview, "We've already solved half of our problems, so we can expect to do well with what remains," will bolster productive action and undercut despair. But if the two partners speak to each other about the situation with the intention of persuading the other to see it their way, neither will feel heard or understood.

Rather than thinking of whether it is more valid to consider the glass half filled or empty, let's consider whether the glass is whole, whether it has integrity. Can the glass serve its function? What is more important, the measure of water it contains at the moment or its design and potential? Will it serve us when it is fuller and when less filled than it is at the moment? Is the present its salient aspect? The glass has not been shattered or crushed. Perhaps this is a more productive tack for evaluation. Rather than accentuating how filled or unfilled it is, perhaps we can focus on whether its potential and function have been preserved. *In many instances, the question is not how much we have but how much we can have, not where are we but how where we are connects us with where we want to be.*

At the Crossroads

Brief case illustration: Daniela and Robin have been together for eleven years. They met when both were in their early twenties. Daniela was considerably more verbal, able to identify and express her feelings clearly, while Robin was hesitant and often unsure about what she felt. Robin admired Daniela's expressiveness. She was attracted to it even while being envious of it.

As their relationship grew, Robin's abilities to understand, identify, and articulate her feelings improved significantly. Unanticipated
difficulties arose.

Previously, Robin could not talk about her anger over how she had
been mistreated in her past, primarily within her family. Robin began
to reconsider many aspects of her life. She wondered whether Daniela
hadn't chosen her in order to feel superior. Did Daniela want her to
become stronger? Robin had occupied the position of the "less capable
one"; now, she pondered whether Daniela had enjoyed the imbalance.
Daniela had accepted Robin as she was—depressed—or, as Robin
expressed it, "when I was so much less than I am now." Robin asked
whether their bond had *depended* on her maintaining the depressed
version of her personality. Having overcome much of her depression,
was there still a secure place for her in their relationship? This exploration upset both partners. Robin accused Daniela of being threatened
by Robin's growth. Daniela felt confused and betrayed.

For this couple to begin to create a middle ground, they had to stop
talking about the glass as being half filled with competitive anger or
half filled with love and take a step back and appreciate that Robin's
self-discoveries were an indication that the relationship itself was a
place in which she was thriving.

Previously, depression colored Robin's life view. Because of the
changes she had made, Robin formed a new way of seeing herself.
Doing so required adjustments and was not easy. Likewise, Daniela
needed to attune herself to the new, less depressed Robin, and this
required adjustments, which were also not easy. However, both were
motivated to make these changes.

There seemed no reason to interpret Daniela's need to adjust as a
sign that she did not support Robin's new strengths. Daniela was challenged by Robin's growth, as was Robin; the challenge was accepted,
not repudiated.

Once the couple could reformulate their idea of what the challenges of the moment meant for them, the middle ground strengthened
dramatically. Robin's anger at Daniela abated, and Daniela's confu-

sion and sense that she had been betrayed softened. A sense of emotional safety began to replace the fear and tension that had menaced their partnership. The glass was neither half filled nor empty, simply intact.

Chapter 7

SEVEN GUIDELINES FOR MIDDLE-GROUND COMMUNICATION

If you need help regulating and resolving conflict safely, these guidelines are for you. They can help you make difficult conversations productive, steer you and your partner away from destructive talk, and help you nurture an atmosphere of emotional safety. Without an atmosphere of emotional safety, nothing flourishes in your relationship except alienation. Adopting these guidelines, whenever pertinent, will safeguard the middle ground within your relationship:

1. Avoid generalizing and stereotyping.
2. Do not blurt responses.
3. No name calling.
4. Speak honestly and judiciously.
5. Develop patience. Sustain it.
6. Think about what your partner says in terms of *who your partner is.*
7. Time-out signal—have it in place; use it as needed.

1. AVOID GENERALIZING AND STEREOTYPING

JOHN: I can't stand being around you when we visit your parents. You *always* get this glazed look in your eyes, and I feel like I'm alone with them.

KAREN: Thanks for the support. At least you're consistent. I can *never* count on you when I'm feeling stressed.

John generalizes about Karen's moods, particularly when she's around her parents. She admits to having a hard time around her parents, but believes that her feelings vary from visit to visit, her concerns change. He speaks about who he thinks she is yet, as far as she's concerned, he doesn't 'get' it. As a result Karen feels neglected and uncared for. She wonders, "Where is his openness to learning more about who I am? Where is his curiosity about who I am with respect to how I feel, as opposed to what he *thinks* I feel?" She adds, "He's got me pigeon-holed. I feel that he takes for granted that he understands me completely even though he doesn't."

Karen belittles John, in turn, by saying that she can "never count on" him when she feels stressed. By counterattacking this way, Karen invalidates whatever helpful efforts John has made at other times. Now he feels minimized and taken for granted. Each partner's sense of emotional safety, as a result of their generalizing, is further diminished.

2. DO NOT BLURT RESPONSES

Do not simply blurt out whatever comes to mind to your partner. Consult *yourself* while speaking with your partner. Do you identify with the following statement: "I didn't even know what I was going to say until I heard myself saying it." If so, this is an especially important guideline for you to work with.

Partners at Square One tend to speak *at* each other without investing energy in listening—to themselves or their partner. The distinction between responding and reacting makes all the difference in creating or destroying middle-ground possibilities.

Important Point: Responding Versus Reacting

Human response—at its most productive—involves reflection. Reacting, like a counter punch, does not. Once a statement is voiced, it cannot be retracted entirely. Impact cannot be recalled. Emphasize the listening aspect of the dialogue in your thinking. Focus on what your partner is expressing about who he is and how he feels. "Listening to yourself as you listen" will help you fan out options and choose your responses with maximum deliberateness and effectiveness.

Mark and Rob are a couple who have been together for four years. I witnessed Mark attempt to repair hurt feelings that developed from an angry exchange they had had over the phone. Mark began with an apology, but Rob quickly derailed the chance for a middle-ground experience with sarcasm. Rob's reactive comments undermine a sense of connection. Let's listen to two versions of the same dialogue.

Version 1

MARK: I'm sorry that the conversation went the way it did. It's very hard for me when we have difficulty communicating.

ROB: Hard for you. That's all you really care about anyway, isn't it? You.

I noted to myself that Rob was making no acknowledgment of Marks's effort to approach him peaceably.

> **MARK** *(beginning to feel defensive)*: That isn't fair, and you know it. I really do get upset when we have those kind of sparring matches on the phone.

> **ROB:** Of course you get upset. Whenever I ask you for anything for me, I can count on you to get upset. Whenever I need something, you disappear.

Mark approaches again, but Rob pushes him away. Far from thinking about how his remarks are affecting the relationship, Rob glories in vindictiveness, driven compulsively by his anger. Reckless and provocative, Rob hurtles on.

> **MARK** *(switching into full defensive mode)*: That isn't true. You know you have a very short memory when it comes to anything positive that I do for you.

> **ROB:** But it isn't as short as your ability to realize when I need to feel like you're there for me, willing to take care of me and be a man about things!

So. Rob goes from accusations of selfishness to attacks on his partner's manhood in three rapid steps.

Before going to guideline 3, let's listen in on an alternate version of their dialogue, this time—with more responding and less reacting.

Version 2

> **MARK:** I'm sorry that the conversation went the way it did. It's very hard for me when we have difficulty communicating.

> **ROB:** Hard for you. That's all you really care about anyway, isn't it?

So far, same as last time around.

> **MARK:** You sound very angry. I'm sorry if I hurt your feelings.

> **ROB:** Why be sorry? I thought people enjoy doing things they do well. About sharing and loving, you know so little, but hurting, that's your area of expertise. I'd think you'd take pride.

Here Mark, rather than beginning to get defensive, senses Rob's upset and does not take Rob's hostility as a personal attack. Rather than investing energy in defending himself, Mark demonstrates concern for Rob by acknowledging Rob's hurt feelings. Rob has accused him of being selfish. He responds by demonstrating generosity and interest. Often, anger masks a plea for connection, and a response that validates this need can be comforting as, here, it soothes Rob.

> **MARK:** I know you must really be angry with me. The only thing I can say is that I'm sorry you feel bad. I want you to feel better.

> **ROB:** Hmmmm . . . *(decidedly softening)*

When Rob becomes angry, it marks the start of a syndrome that characteristically causes him to feel out of control. By pursuing Rob's need for connection and attention, Mark creates a bridge that underscores his understanding of how difficult this out-of-control feeling is for Rob. This helps Rob feel less isolated, which soothes him. Mark's response models the opposite of belittling Rob's feelings. By daring to approach Rob directly, Mark demonstrates confidence that order can be restored to their chaotic interchange. His offer of tender contact is accepted. Through his initiative, Mark has located the middle ground, and Rob extends himself beyond the confines of his anger to join him there.

MARK: Whatever I've done that's upset you, I'm sorry that you are upset.

ROB: I probably didn't need to get that angry. I know there was no reason for it.

Here, Mark's apology acknowledges and expresses concern for his partner's pain. Rob's reply signals that he is relieved to feel less isolated; his reflective side emerges, no longer eclipsed by the anger. Research indicates that couples who can resolve anger together, as Rob and Mark do in this second version of their fight, have a good prognosis for success as a couple.

Rob's comments during the first version of their fight were inappropriate to the needs of their relationship. The only sense in which his remarks were appropriate is that they segue perfectly into our next guideline.

3. NO NAME CALLING

Amy Flynn, my son's beloved nursery school teacher, makes this pitch to her preschoolers year after year. Adjusted for adults it goes like this: If you are disgusted with something that is going on and call your mate *a jerk*, *a bitch*, *a fat slob*, *irresponsible*, *idiotic*, *disgusting*, and so on, the communication flow stops. And turning it back on will be a feat. When thinking before speaking, edit out the put-downs. Basic as the guidelines may seem, under stress, sticking to them is a challenge for us all.

4. SPEAK HONESTLY AND JUDICIOUSLY

Although I caution above against blurting out perceptions that have not been sufficiently thought out, the abiding ways that you feel—

positive and negative—need to be represented in your dialogue with your partner. Keeping dominant thoughts and feelings buried will not further the relationship.

The question is *how* to convey these messages. Particularly "hot" or inflamed topics require equal measures of finesse and forethought.

This does not mean that every thought or feeling must eventually be expressed. Rule of thumb is: you need to be known by and know your partner. And your partner needs to be known by and know you. Having said that, I believe you are entitled—and in some instances obligated—to keep certain things private if exposing them will *only* promote pain and serve no constructive purpose.

Think before you speak. Speak honestly and judiciously.

5. DEVELOP PATIENCE. SUSTAIN IT.

Find a way to take actual or metaphorical deep breaths when you are under stress. Practice the exercises, miniexercises, and tips in this book; in varying ways they all help extend patience.

One of my goals is to help you think through your own messages and be as available as possible to listen to and think about your partner's. Without patience, this important goal is drastically compromised. *Patience within a specific talk and in the pacing of your dialogue overall can make a critical difference to relationship healing.* Patience and humility blended together compose emotional stamina, which is fundamental to the creation of a secure long-term love relationship.

Paradoxically, patience functions as a catalyst for the process of mutual understanding; without patience dialogue cannot progress along its natural, step-wise course. Acts of impatience stem the flow of middle-ground communication, causing temporary paralysis or, worse, irreparable disruption. Don't take on the impossible. Healing without patience? Impossible.

6. THINK ABOUT WHAT YOUR PARTNER SAYS IN TERMS OF *WHO YOUR PARTNER IS*

I'm not recommending that you relinquish your own perspective. You need to develop a "relationship" perspective that features a good grasp of how the situation is understood by your partner *as well as* by yourself. This perspective generates and affirms the middle ground. Achieving this step takes determination. Remember—understanding how your partner feels from within his or her purview does not mean you are acknowledging that this perspective is correct. You are not surrendering your point of view. You are simply acknowledging that it is not the only legitimate point of view.

7. TIME-OUT SIGNAL—HAVE IT IN PLACE; USE IT AS NEEDED

Complex issues need to be broken down into manageable chunks. To do this, you've got to have a way to punctuate the boundaries between the related, but separate, stages of dialogue. Without a method for temporarily discontinuing the talk, getting restarted can feel too overwhelming to even attempt.

Using time-outs can allow you a sense of control in the pacing of your dialogue. In the case of complex and/or difficult emotional issues this can make the difference between whether you can or can't discuss an issue productively. Without a prearranged signal to allow a safe method for temporarily suspending the dialogue, restarting it will be more difficult.

Recommendation: Devise your time-out signal together if possible. It can be as simple as raising a finger on either hand or more elaborate if you wish. Prepare yourself to respond graciously if your partner should voice need for a time-out. Using time-outs does not mean that difficult issues go unaddressed. It does mean that partners have to work as a team to keep the flow of conversation going—not simply within a single talk but between talks as well. Carve a niche in your relationship that honors this dimension of awareness and sensitivity.

Illustrating the Time-Out

Vickie and Damian were in the midst of a heated and often explosive marital impasse when they began couples' therapy with me. Damian acknowledged having had an affair but said that, if it were possible, he wanted to work out his relationship with Vickie.

Vickie felt unable to talk with him about anything without becoming enraged and verbally abusive. She seemed to become equally enraged when accusing him of leaving the cap off the toothpaste as when discussing his having had the affair. She described her situation this way: "I'm unwilling to open any of this up, even though I realize that without discussing it, it's festering and the anger is going to continue and probably grow. I keep feeling that any attempt at talking about our feelings may bring the relationship to an end."

Vickie now was hypersensitized to any interaction that was angry or even threatened to become angry. To avoid overreacting, she tried to avoid communicating completely. This created its own set of problems.

I coached Vickie and Damian to devise a time-out signal. Vickie was able to begin talking about some of what was on her mind. Points of connection began to be reestablished. Using these time-outs, Vickie was able to *slow herself down*. Knowing that she could signal a time-out bolstered Vickie's sense of self-control in the couple's dialogue.

New understandings began to grow. After a time-out, Vickie could get in touch with how hurt she was and talk about these feelings rather than railing about the toothpaste cap or some other unfinished chore. Damian, to his credit, was able to listen to her, take in the depth of pain she was experiencing.

Reciprocally, Damian sometimes felt confused about some of the ambivalent feelings that had led him to have an affair. Although he did not feel good about having betrayed Vickie, he harbored anger toward her for her part in creating the situation that had, in his words, "made him look outside the relationship for sex and affection." He felt that he could have made different choices but, at the same time, also felt Vickie could have done a better job of handling her own options. At times, he used the time-out signal to collect himself, to differentiate between what needed to be discussed with Vickie and what he needed to work through privately.

This simple technique—calling a time-out—kept their interactions safer. They needed their dialogue to resume *gradually*, and the time-outs provided structure that allowed them to regulate the rhythm and intensity of their talks.

Can following the guidelines in this chapter save a floundering relationship? The short answer is yes. If you follow them consistently, you will see results.

EXERCISE: GUIDELINE MASTERY QUIZ

Rate your attitude to the following on a scale of 1 to 5, where 5 means you agree strongly and 1 means you strongly disagree. You and your partner should write your answers on separate sheets of paper. Then, follow the instructions under "Scoring Procedure" to see where you stand.

1. ___ Within the past eight months, I have *not* called my partner by an unflattering name (such as "stupid," "bitch," "bastard") once.
2. ___ Within the past eight months, I have called my partner by an unflattering name (such as "stupid," "bitch," "bastard") one or more times.
3. ___ Very rarely have I found myself speaking without thinking about what I am saying.
4. ___ I believe in saying what I feel when I feel it, and letting the chips fall where they may.

5. ___ Patience is a problem for me, but I can pull myself together and exhibit patience when it is required.
6. ___ No matter what I do, I cannot hold my tongue when I get angry.
7. ___ I recognize that my partner sometimes expresses himself or herself in a way that doesn't really do justice to the way he or she feels or thinks.
8. ___ I do not believe that my partner is capable of changing the way he or she thinks or expresses himself or herself.
9. ___ If my partner were to tell me he or she needs a "time-out" while we are talking, I would respect this and be ready to arrange another time to continue the conversation.
10. ___ If my partner were to tell me he or she needs a "time-out" while we are talking, I would feel offended and do what I could to keep the conversation going in the moment.

Scoring Procedure

1. Total the number of points for even-numbered questions and for odd-numbered questions separately.
2. Subtract the largest score total from the other score total. For example, if odd-numbered questions total 20, and the even-numbered questions total is 10, subtract the even total (10) from the odd total (20). The score you have then is 10, with odd-greater. If even questions totaled 36, and odd questions totaled 18, the result would be 18 even-greater.

Charting Results

For odd-greater scores: Scores of 0–9 indicate that you have absorbed some of the guideline principles but are committed to ideas that cause difficulties in creating middle-ground dialogue as well. I strongly advise you to review the guidelines and spend time thinking about and working on the "Guideline Review" exercise that follows this quiz.

Scores of 10–18 indicate that you have absorbed the majority of the guidelines. It will be important for you to clarify for yourself which guidelines are most problematic and work with yourself to become as aware as possible of when these behaviors, actions, or attitudes negatively affect your relationship. Scores of 18 or above indicate a firm grasp of the guidelines presented.

For even-greater scores: Scores of 0–9 indicate that you probably have difficulty controlling your anger, thinking before speaking, and/or granting your partner the benefit of the doubt for the sake of encouraging an open dialogue. Review the guidelines carefully, and in working on the "Guideline Review" exercise that follows this quiz. I recommend that you attempt to keep a journal to track your attempts to implement these middle-ground guidelines. Improving your grasp of these concepts will be important in creating a middle ground with your partner. Scores of 10–18 indicate that your difficulty controlling your anger is fairly severe. You may consider yourself an impatient person. You may experience despair at the possibility of gaining greater control of your anger or of working through difficulties with your partner. The good news is that the guidelines are clear and straightforward. If you work with yourself, you can make significant changes. It will be important for you to keep a journal or, if you do not think you could keep a journal, figure out a method of prompting yourself to become increasingly conscious of how you handle your anger and your attitude toward your partner when you try to discuss any issue. Do you allow for disagreements? Do you find that you are continuously disappointed and angry with your partner? Read over the exercises in this book—especially the "Basic Three-Step," "Reaching Out from the Inside," and "One Talks, the Other Doesn't." Scores of 18 or above indicate that you need a wake-up call. It seems that you are angry much of the time and tend to be impatient and intolerant of your partner. Go over the guidelines carefully. Read over the suggestions made above; they can help you strengthen your communication skills. If you work with the concept of the middle ground and the exercises, you can make great progress.

EXERCISE: GUIDELINE REVIEW

Of the seven guidelines discussed in this chapter, is there one that is most relevant to your relationship?

1. Avoid generalizing and stereotyping.
2. Do not blurt responses.
3. No name calling.
4. Speak honestly and judiciously.
5. Develop patience. Sustain it.
6. Think about what your partner says in terms of *who your partner is.*
7. Time-out signal—have it in place; use it as needed.

Take a moment to jot down some thoughts about the guideline that poses the greatest problem in your relationship *for you*—in terms of your actions and behavior. Try and explain as best you can why this is so.

_____

_____

_____

_____

_____

_____

_____

_____

Jot down your thoughts on which guideline is most problematic in your partner's actions and behaviors. Explain how you understand your partner's actions and behaviors in terms of who he or she is as a person as best you can.

_____

_____

_____

_____

_____

_____

_____

_____

Give yourself a moment to reflect on how your relationship would change if you could incorporate these guidelines into your interactions *most* of the time. Take a few minutes to formulate your thoughts on the lines below.

_____

_____

_____

_____

_____

_____

_____

_____

Chapter 8

LETTING GO OF ANGER

ANGER—A CHALLENGE
TO THE MIDDLE GROUND

Many couples have difficulty handling anger. Middle-ground connections often get forged as work on anger proceeds. How does anger function in a relationship? Is it always a destructive force? Is it sometimes a catalyst of the change process? Anger can function differently at different times within a relationship. In addition, couples bring their idiosyncratic history of resolved and unresolved experiences with anger in their parents' home—some of which may be helpful to them in their relationship and some of which may be problematic.

The Story of Carl and Amanda

Let's observe Amanda and Carl, at home in their apartment, tune into a television program. Amanda turns toward Carl and remarks that the TV news commentator has lightened her hair. Carl replies, "I didn't notice." His disinterest in the show, Amanda insists, typifies his disinterest in sharing experience with her generally; she accuses him of being "self-involved" and "uncaring."

He counterattacks. "Why is it that whenever you have something to say to me, it's a criticism?"

The anger escalates.

She adds, "You only notice what you want to notice, and you don't care about what anybody else notices. If I pull your attention to anything you hadn't been thinking of on your own, you don't participate. I'm alone, and I'm sick and tired of being alone."

To which Carl responds, "The reason you feel alone is because your idea of a conversation is picking me apart. Whatever I say, it's wrong."

There is no history of dialogue within their relationship to which they can return to strengthen a sense of mutuality; none exists. Disappointment crowds out exploratory, explanatory, or clarifying talk. Impatience dictates the pace and content of what they say to one another and how they say it.

Impatience

For his part, Carl's impatience results in explosive outbursts followed by withdrawal. His reactive style of anger is problematic. Their dance had become a fixed sequence: her mistrust triggers his rage, which leads her to feel victimized and misunderstood; this confirms his despair which produces angry outbursts or, alternately, withdrawal.

Consider the argument that erupted between them while watching the news. Their dance of anger, as Harriet Lerner discusses extensively in her numerous helpful books (see *The Dance of Anger*), destroys chances for healing, not because it centers on anger, but because the rigid sequence forecloses possibilities for working creatively to resolve disagreements or even air differences productively.

Stable couples tend to resolve difficulties. Troubled couples are in trouble, in large measure, because they can't. Research backs the notion that, among married couples, inability to resolve anger, rather

than the occurrence of angry scenes within a relationship, is a significant predictor of marital failure. It isn't a question of whether a couple
fights but of whether they can resolve their fights.

The Dark-Adapted Eye

In one of her popular mystery novels, *The Dark-Adapted Eye*, Barbara
Vine writes of a condition that develops when no light is available to
someone for an extended time. The affected person loses tolerance for
light so that, although the potential for sight itself has not been damaged, she is functionally blind.

The condition, dark-adapted eye, is remediable, but its therapy
requires the patient to tolerate a change process that brings discomfort
and requires patience. A patient's natural tendency to resist giving up
the comfort of darkness stymies healing.

For couples like Amanda and Carl to exchange their bleak outlook
for a brighter, more satisfying life together, they must brave changes.
This takes willingness to bear some discomfort in acclimating themselves to a new outlook.

As continued darkness offers no hope for regaining normal sight
to the dark-adapted eye, inability to grapple with the change process
rules out possibilities for healing once problems have become
entrenched.

The Sneer behind the Smile

When Carl smiled at Amanda, she interpreted his smile as either
mocking or sardonic.

John Gottman coined a handy term, "positive override," which
refers to the ability of one's partner to interpret an interaction positively. It is very much like giving your partner the benefit of the doubt
or, taken a step further, like not even having a doubt but automatically
crediting your partner with good intentions even when his or her
behavior may be questionable. For example, Lee, husband of Jean, a

couple whose interactions will be discussed later in the book, made a joke about her singing. "Positive override" allowed her to interpret his comment as a joke, maybe not that funny, but not something to be taken as serious criticism—not a sign of his mistreating her or not appreciating her as a person. She did not take offense.

Carl and Amanda's interactions exemplify an opposite trend: "negative override." Even when Carl was genuinely glad to see her, Amanda read his smile as ridicule. I worked to help Amanda allow for the *possibility* that, *some* of the time, she *might* be misconstruing Carl's smile. I believe I saw a variety of meanings in his smiles, while she saw only one. Negative override.

I did not try dissuading Amanda from her belief that there were times that his smile was unfriendly. I did not doubt that this might be so—at times. However, since her expectations had become fixed, she was functionally blind—not just resistant—to noticing if his expressions, particularly his smile, held any other qualities. She seemed unable to even consider that a different quality might exist in Carl's current or potential emotional range.

In the beginning of our work together, Amanda could not extend any credibility to the idea that Carl had agreed to participate in couples' therapy because he wanted the relationship to improve. Exploration of the rigidity with which she held this anger required careful examination; both the anger and the rigidity posed formidable obstacles to healing.

Negative Attention Span

Habituation to single-second jump cuts and myriad other truncated experiences—pervasive in our culture—have created our much-publicized short attention span. The media direct us through countless discrete images. In witnessing a nearly continuous barrage of disjointed sequences, the mind numbs at the prospect of pulling it all together into a cohesive message. We are not conditioned to attend to the meaning of what we witness, but rather to the sensation brought on by what we see. In other words, we are acculturated to react quickly to quickly changing stimuli and to react by gauging our sensations, not by reflecting on our experience.

An extended gaze coupled with a reflective posture, directed at either an image or a relationship, stands in decided contrast with these hi-tech times. We are not a contemplative society. Many partners, however, move beyond the style of perception and discourse that is dominated by a short attention span. They develop what I call a "negative attention span": they become proficient at forgetting what the other is *about* to say.

Holding other's statements in mind and building their communication toward a composite understanding of who they are and what their communications mean is part of a process that requires an expanded attention span.

Amanda, as many angry partners do, had cultivated this style to such a degree that Carl had virtually no chance of getting a message or idea across with her.

Is this situation applicable to your own? Have you noticed yourself or your partner jump to conclusions, dismissing the other's statements before *they are completed? Or get angry before what you suspect may have happened is verified as having occurred?*

Negative attention span, a condition that has struck many contemporary couples, is lethal to dialogue because if something new is ventured, the chances that the new element will be appreciated diminish greatly. Opportunities for the middle ground tend to be missed.

> **Food for thought:** Do you get into repetitive arguments that go nowhere? If so, reflect on whether you share Amanda's tendency to prejudge, rather than listen to, her partner.

Brief Notes on Anger

Anger in itself may or may not be problematic. As stated elsewhere, anger, even frequent arguing in itself, is not necessarily a sign that a relationship is troubled. Often the intensity of anger reflects the strength of the desire to connect and the frustration of not being able to. For some couples, then, frequent fights are proportionate to their passionate commitment to working things out. Anger *with poor resolution* signifies relationship trouble.

Your anger style—and expectations about whether anger can or cannot get resolved with your partner—is shaped by family experiences and temperament. Creating and discussing anger genograms (a fuller discussion of genograms is provided toward the end of this chapter) illuminates these family patterns of anger. Both partners learn what they are "up against" when attempting to handle the challenge of interpersonal anger. This technique has helped couples create mutual insight and a shared experience related to their histories and patterns of dealing with anger.

Breakthrough

As therapy progressed, Amanda developed the ability to interpret Carl's smile and other gestures more flexibly. She became able to question her own interpretation of Carl's smile as a sneer.

During a session, Carl appeared to me to be genuinely disconcerted when Amanda claimed that he was looking scornfully at her. He replied that he had been feeling sympathetic and interested in what she was saying at that moment. Amanda was able to give Carl the benefit of the doubt in this instance; this proved an important step in their relationship. Her ability to reflect on her own perception of his feeling state was a key advance for her personally. She was reclaiming her capacity to reflect on her feelings, something once incapacitated by the intensity of her anger.

Progress

This step, combined with Carl's work on his style of handling his anger, signaled a stage of growth in which possibilities for a middle ground emerged. My work with Carl in toning down his fiery temper, in helping him develop more flexibility in his handling of *his* anger, enabled him to participate in increasing possibilities for connection.

Food for thought:

- How often in your disagreements with your partner are you able to take in what is being said and entertain an explanation that does not coincide with what you originally had thought about the situation?
- If you can do this, you've got the basis for a middle-ground dialogue. If not, note this as an issue that may need to be worked with.
- Remember, if you cannot accept and discuss ideas or opinions that differ from your own, the likelihood is that your partner will not extend that acceptance back to you when you wish to communicate something that he or she does not agree with you about.
- To break this cycle, someone's got to extend the benefit of the doubt to the other; breaking this pattern dramatically improves chances for mutuality.

RESOLVING THE PAST

In couples' sessions, we explored the triggers and causes of Carl's explosive anger, which turned out to be part of a psychological strategy—you could call it a defense—against acknowledging feelings of helplessness or depression or both. When these feelings registered, unconsciously, rather than experiencing himself as feeling helpless or depressed, he convulsed in a fit of anger. The anger became highly visible. All, including himself, were distracted from identifying the underlying feeling states. This gave Carl a temporary sense of control over these deeper feelings but also prevented him from resolving them. Much of these feelings stemmed from experiences within his family. You might ask, "Why hadn't anyone noticed Carl's inability to resolve his sadness?" A good question, but undiagnosed depression in men is widespread. It remains invisible to most of us, including the men who suffer with it.

Changes Bring Changes

Amanda began to grow more curious and patient with Carl; he became more three-dimensional to her. She prejudged him less and became a more accurate and empathic listener. Her negative attention span let up. This increased opportunities for them to make meaningful contact.

Although Amanda had insisted that they come for couples' therapy, she had also held onto the contradictory position that nothing would help. This "belief" spoke directly to her underlying despair about being able to work things through and to her sorrowful desperation about establishing a secure attachment with Carl.

Understanding Brings Empathy

Amanda, in witnessing Carl work with difficult feelings related to his family of origin, found it hard to continue attributing the meaning of all his actions to what had gone on between them. She began to see that much of the anger and confusion that she'd taken personally had origins elsewhere. She spoke of her own chronic feelings of being unappreciated and taken for granted in terms of her own family of origin. She no longer cast Carl as the villain responsible for the existence of all her painful emotions.

The youngest of two daughters, Amanda felt her parents invested their emotional energy in her sister and treated Amanda as an afterthought, never the main concern. She recalled feeling appreciated only when she amused herself or, in some other way, eliminated the need for her parents to focus on her. With her parents, much of the time, Amanda felt a need for more attention than she received. Because her parents seemed to value her most when she did not follow her impulse to seek more attention, she felt bound in a contradiction: either she was true to herself and earned parental disapproval or she disregarded her needs and won their approval. This resulted in her feeling conflicted and anxiety-ridden through much of her childhood and adolescence.

She acknowledged difficulty envisioning Carl, or anyone, taking her feelings seriously—as their main concern. This was a problem that Amanda had carried into the relationship with her. Issues involving what may have seemed to be "surface communication"—like Amanda's interpretation of Carl's smile—so often connect to deeper, more essential issues, like despair. I wondered about Amanda's basic temperament. Did she have a genetic predisposition toward feeling depressed that had been actuated by the stress of family conflict? There was now a legitimate space in our work—and in their relationship—to explore these important issues.

Modulating Anger: What Makes It So Hard?

Carl's father was soft-spoken, essentially nonverbal; his mother filled the room with wishes and commands. Carl's hot temper was patterned on hers. He felt his mother bullied him and his father.

According to Carl, "I wanted to see my father take care of himself. My mother talked him down at every turn. He'd give in. I didn't want to be like that."

When he felt Amanda was getting the upper hand in an argument, Carl refused to cave in quietly. Instead, he'd explode. To Carl, the blowups burst him free of becoming a clone of his father. This explains at least some of why Carl was so resolute when angered, accounts for his ferocious resistance to changing this pattern, and touches on why his anger escalated so quickly into rage.

When we are angered, associations drawn from early experience form the basis upon which we understand our options. We sometimes fail to enact commonsense responses and instead favor inappropriate acts, in part because these commonsense responses have not been integrated into our understanding as viable options. The pull to react angrily in the style that represents our family background is typically triggered outside our conscious awareness. This is why changing anger patterns is so difficult. Genetic factors complicate the picture further.

Understanding Carl's Anger and His Father's

It took some time to help Carl see that the expression of anger that he felt his father could not bring himself to make, but that Carl felt his father needed to have made, was not equivalent to his own angry responses to Amanda. From what Carl told me, I came to believe that his father had swallowed angry responses that would have helped his parents understand each other better, had his father spoken his mind. Rather than withdraw into silence, if his father had made his anger explicit, that anger may have served a connective function between Carl's parents. His father's lack of overt anger represented nonresponsiveness to Carl's mother. His father was passive in that sense.

Carl's knee-jerk anger, predictable and routine, induced a pattern of disconnection. His chronic outbursts with Amanda—which signified interpersonal paralysis rather than breakthrough—represented avoidance of the challenge to take *meaningful* action; that meaningful action needed to involve sensitive listening to what her criticisms entailed.

Carl had already proved to himself and the world that he could take a stand. He now needed to prove to himself and the world that he could allow himself the freedom to listen patiently to his partner.

Carl's Challenge

Carl's personal challenges could no longer be based on the fantasies that he'd had as a boy or younger man. Although unaware of it, he had outgrown all that.

Simply reversing what he saw as his father's style—as an inhibitor of anger—would not solve the communication problems Carl faced with Amanda. His relationship with Amanda posed a *developmental* challenge to him.

To break new ground, Carl would have to bring his focus on relational challenge into the present. Previously, without understanding the influence of his family, he had been stuck in the rigid pattern of explosiveness. With greater awareness and support, middle-ground areas emerged between himself and Amanda. The outbursts decreased in frequency and intensity.

Emphasizing Connection

Carl had wanted to be respected as a strong man whose voice could not be silenced. He, however, failed to grasp that Amanda was coming at him with great force and persistence because he had *already* achieved such a powerful presence in their relationship and in her life. Carl's continued push to be perceived as strong was sheer overkill.

Now he needed to hold onto Amanda's total message and convey to her that he had grasped it. Her criticisms contained her longing for a healthier, more secure connection with him. And along with that longing, her rage, desperation, and frustration were based on how difficult securing this connection was.

Also, her criticisms were meant, taken in their most productive direction, to prompt him to participate in the relationship differently. Amanda's venting dissatisfaction with the state of the relationship was positive for them both; she was fighting to include him in something that was more than what they had *because* what they had was not enough for either of them.

Carl needed to understand the sense in which she was continuing, despite all the rancor, to act as his ally or, at the least, potential ally. Carl needed to acknowledge Amanda's strength in persevering to connect with him. Her criticism, ultimately, was centered on helping him expand his repertoire of emotional responses beyond anger and withdrawal.

New understandings made it possible for Carl to reduce his own anger considerably. He began to see her criticism, as described above, as a demonstration of his importance to her; the heat of her anger, a sign of her passion for connecting with him.

Gradually, Amanda began to feel better understood. As the feeling of being heard and understood increased, the level of desperation about maintaining a connection decreased, and, overall, the mood between them improved.

Solutions Are Complex Because Feelings Are Complex

But Carl still felt caught in a bind. Though he had always felt his father should have "stood up for himself" in arguments with his mother, Carl realized, as the therapy progressed, that he also had idealized his father's failure to take a strong stand.

Though self-contradictory, Carl realized that he had felt his dad, in *not* retaliating against Carl's mother, had acted selflessly, sparing her the pain of confrontation, an act of manly self-sacrifice. Although this contradicted other feelings, Carl nonetheless came to see that he held this feeling strongly.

How is it that Carl thought his father weak for his silence and, at the same time, idealized that same silence as a demonstration of strength?

The concept of "ambivalence"—holding a feeling and the polar opposite of that same feeling simultaneously—is firmly entrenched in the history of psychoanalytic tradition. Sigmund Freud believed that all emotions are held with degrees of ambivalence. Often, one is conscious of one aspect of an emotion but not the other. Carl gradually became aware of both sides of his ambivalence toward his father and so, importantly, was able to explore both aspects of himself.

Pushover or Saint?

Carl began to experience internal pressure to be with Amanda the way his dad had been with his mother. Still, he couldn't come to terms with whether his father had been a pushover or a saint. Carl seemed to get to know himself better and in the process become more, instead of less, confused.

Carl's expressing his anger openly both connected him to the potential he sensed in his father and also alienated him from the part of himself that saw his father's silence as a sign of kindness. Carl's understanding of his own and others' emotional makeup was becoming increasingly complex, much more adult than it had been previously.

Gaining awareness of these conflicts and confusions in itself, which helped hold the volatility of his anger in place, took some pressure off Carl. Pulled in contradictory directions, he was pinned to a state of dynamic tension. Uncovering the complexity of his issues helped him regain control over how he handled his anger. Rather than struggling to reconcile internal inconsistencies, Carl grew better able to accept them as aspects of a richer inner life. He anguished less about the need to choose which inclinations he wished to follow. Rather than simply reacting, he became aware of having choices to make.

A Shared Myth

Carl and Amanda, in their lives outside therapy, both prided themselves on holding high opinions of their parents. Both shared the following myth: good people don't criticize their parents. Both identified with the feeling that if people do criticize their parents, they are unappreciative and disloyal. Amanda and Carl came to see that noticing problems in their parents and in their parents' relationship was not the same thing as devaluing their familial heritage. Ultimately, they realized that feeling free to understand how their parents had interacted with them was a way of fulfilling their parents' greatest hope for them—that they become adults and take control of their own lives to the fullest extent possible.

Progressively understanding their parents' communication helped them feel freer to get clearer about their own. This clarity became a basis of a new middle ground, a new beginning. Dialogue between them, in which their parents' relationships were viewed critically when appropriate, became possible without their feeling that they were doing something wrong. This resulted, as it so often does, with them feeling more compassion for their parents, who had suffered relational strife similar to their own. They also began to feel more compassion toward each other.

A New Home Base

Overcoming denial of problems in their parents' relationships had positive ramifications for them both. The repetitive "dance" of blame–accusation–retaliation did not disappear entirely but diminished. Fewer disagreements became fights. Feelings of loneliness ebbed, though both had become aware of a need to build more support for themselves outside as well as inside their relationship.

Regression to their former patterns threatened during times of stress. When this occurred, the feeling was less "Here we are again, stuck back at home base" and more "How did we get back here? This isn't home base anymore."

They listened to each other better. They were able to reapproach each other and resolve fights more effectively. A way to talk with each other, not just at each other, evolved. They had come a long way from when Carl's lack of interest in the TV commentator's change in hair color sparked a vehement argument that left them both bruised and despairing.

First Step toward Healing

The first step along the journey is to lose the way, the old way—argument compounded upon argument, disappointment upon disappointment—that has been leading nowhere. You need to discover possibilities for doing things differently, achieving different outcomes.

At the beginning of our work together, Amanda had said, "Something is missing between us. We both probably know that, but we don't know how to talk about it or what to do." In my practice as a couples' therapist, I hear variations of this theme—"something's missing between us"—from many couples.

Amanda asked, "Why do we repeat the same argument over and over? It doesn't seem to matter what we're talking about. It all feels the same. The fight seems to have a life of its own." With no resolution, chronic anger drains energy needed for creating a middle ground.

EXERCISE: YOUR ANGER PROFILE

Introduction

This exercise provides a structured way to think through and learn about aspects of your own and—if you share the questionnaire results—your partner's style and history related to the issue of anger. This topic is often not fully explored in couples' lives and couples' work so the exercise and subsequent discussions—if you have them—may yield surprises that must be handled with sensitivity and tact. If you can do so: compare and contrast your histories and comfort levels with the expression and experience of anger; this will increase your ability to understand life from your partner's viewpoint.

Patterns of anger typically form outside of awareness of what they are or how they affect relationships. Becoming increasingly conscious of these patterns makes it more possible to modify aspects that are problematic.

The numerical score for each individual questionnaire item is meant to be a key element of the 'food for thought' that this exercise provides. No cumulative scores are attainable. The exercise is designed this way to emphasize the nonjudgmental mindset with which analysis of differences in style—and responses to test items—needs to be understood and discussed.

Immediately following the questionnaire, you'll find a brief worksheet designed to help you organize your responses to the questionnaire.

If you find the topic of anger too volatile to approach without a third party in the room, then I recommend you try it in the presence of a qualified couples therapist.

The Anger Questionnaire.

Rate your attitude to the following on a scale of 1 to 5, where 5 means you agree strongly and 1 means you strongly disagree. You and your partner should write your answers on separate sheets of paper.

Note: Some questions involve use of alcohol. In responding, consider the term "alcohol" as a catchall category that includes and applies to use of alcohol and/or any other substances, including marijuana.

1. I sometimes raise my voice to express myself without being aware I am doing so.
2. I avoid speaking about charged or conflictual topics.
3. It takes an awful lot to make me express anger or disapproval.
4. Growing up in my family, I learned that if something bothers me, it's always better to wait until the problem passes than to speak about it.
5. Sarcasm is unusual for me.
6. When I drink, I am more likely to get into angry arguments.
7. When I was growing up, in my family, the only person who showed open anger was my father.
8. My mother tended to avoid raising her voice in anger but frequently criticized and disapproved of me.
9. There are two types of individuals—people who anger easily and those who are cool no matter what happens.
10. My partner and I don't mind arguing because making up usually feels good.
11. My partner and I argue frequently, and nothing ever gets resolved.
12. I have said many hurtful things to my partner that I wish I could take back.
13. I wish I could hold my breath or count to ten before blowing my top. For me, that seems impossible.
14. I tend to withdraw after I drink anything alcoholic. My

partner finds this annoying, so when I drink, we usually end up arguing.

15. My parents modeled clear articulation of angry feelings.

16. Anger was taboo as a topic of conversation in my home.

17. When I was growing up, disagreements were not voiced in conversations. Angry feelings were expressed through yelling, screaming.

18. Most often, angry feelings were "swallowed."

19. Only one of my parents expressed anger openly. The other tended to withdraw in the face of anger.

20. It is equally difficult for me to express anger as it is to express more positive feelings.

21. I have a much easier time expressing positive feelings than negative ones.

Anger Worksheet

Based on my responses to the questionnaire, I believe that my greatest strength in dealing with anger is:

_____
_____
_____
_____
_____

I believe that my greatest weakness in dealing with anger is:

_____
_____
_____
_____
_____

I believe my partner's greatest strength in dealing with anger is:

_____

_____

_____

_____

_____

I believe my partner's greatest weakness in dealing with anger is:

_____

_____

_____

_____

_____

Together, our greatest challenge in dealing with anger is:

_____

_____

_____

_____

_____

EXERCISE: YOUR ANGER GENOGRAM

Introduction

Although this exercise can be done without having completed the anger questionnaire, working through the questionnaire prior to the genogram is recommended.

I suggest that you and your partner create anger genograms, each working on your own separately. After completing them, share and discuss. Caveat: as with the anger questionnaire, if this activity escalates anger, attempt it in the presence of a couples' therapist.

What Is a Genogram?

A genogram (see illustration on p. 186), a family tree, systematizes the recording of family structure and history. Information like birth order, patterns of relative closeness/distance between family members, incidences of alcohol and/or drug use, and so on, are placed strategically within a diagram. Individuals' professions/occupations, dates of marriage/divorce, talents, learning problems, dominant character traits or temperament, and other outstanding family issues can also regularly be charted.

Some of this information is indicated by standard symbols, which are listed below in the genogram legend. Each genogram can be individualized to suit specific educational or clinical purposes. When you do your own, if possible, include at least three generations. Data included on genograms should be selected judiciously to heighten clarity.

Example: Ida through Lisa to Charlotte

Grandparents' traits often resurface in grandchildren's lives, sometimes bypassing the generation of parents in between. For example, Lisa's mother, Ida, was bossy and short-tempered. One of three siblings and the only girl, Ida was not encouraged to go to college, though both her brothers were and did. Her resentment about this colored much of her life.

As a mother, Ida was impatient with Lisa and stifled the girl's attempts at self-expressiveness. Lisa felt unable to rebel openly against Ida, but when she became a mother, encouraged her daughter, Charlotte, to express her thoughts and feelings emphatically, as if to compensate for the lack of encouragement Charlotte had received from Ida.

Lisa went so far as to support and nurture Charlotte's feeling that she was entitled to command the center of attention in virtually any social situation. Lisa also validated Charlotte's "right" to protest if anyone challenged this sense of entitlement. Charlotte, consequently, developed the habit and reputation of being bossy and short-tempered if she didn't get her way. Relatives observed that Charlotte's personality was a carbon copy of her maternal grandmother, Ida. We can trace the intergenerational transmission of a domineering personality style in this family. Biology may have contributed as well; there is no reason to rule this possibility out.

Lisa and Sam came to me for couples' therapy because of disagreement about how the children's relative needs for attention were being handled. Sam, Lisa's husband and Charlotte's father, felt that Charlotte

SAMPLE ANGER GENOGRAM:

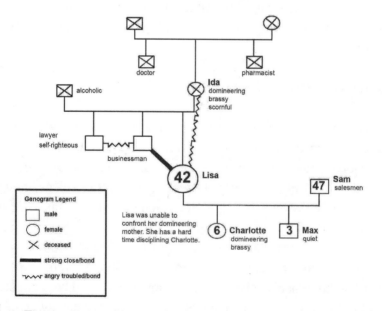

Note: The genogram does not include a great many details about family life. Select, so as to highlight, the facts most relevant to the theme of anger in your family as you work on your own family genogram.

was being indulged too much, while Max, their youngest child, was, compared with Charlotte, not getting his fair share of attention.

As a result of our work with the genogram, Lisa began to grasp a connection between her feeling submerged by Ida's anger and her insistence that Charlotte be given "the share of the spotlight that I never had." Lisa could see that her own unresolved anger toward Ida had colored her judgment. Though Lisa felt she had been supporting Charlotte, she began to see that, by not setting limits for her or teaching her to respect the rights of others with whom she interacted, Lisa was setting Charlotte up to have serious problems in connecting with people—as her mother, Ida, did.

Now, on separate sheets of paper, I recommend you and your partner create your own anger genograms. Sharing results of each other's drawings presents a rich opportunity for you both to learn about and support each other's self-exploration. If you do discuss your genograms, it is important to do so with compassion and nonjudgmental acceptance.

Chapter 9

TWO MYTHS

I remember talking with my sister, Linda, about boy-girl relationships. She was fifteen and obsessed with Bob H., a classmate. I was about seven, preoccupied with baseball, stickball, comic books, and candy.

Back and forth across the dining room table, she traded her blend of investigative questions and pearls of wisdom for my short phrases and blank stares. Bravado masked any doubts she may have felt about her subject; she was characteristically earnest and self-assured. She needed to fill me—her empty vessel of a brother—with her overflow of newly acquired understanding.

"What do you do when you want to meet someone?" she asked.

"Someone like who?" I replied, probably sounding a little suspicious. In all likelihood, I expected she might be leading me down the garden path into some version of knock-knock joke.

"Let's say there is a girl that you'd like to say hello to. What do you do?" I observed her warily.

She continued without prompting. "You walk over and start talking."

I wasn't in the habit of walking up to people that I didn't know. This struck me as a peculiar idea.

"Two people who are attracted to each other begin a conversation—that's the most natural thing in the world. And from there, things just happen; they work out. They get to know each other. That's the way it is." Conviction about the inevitability of this process was unmistakable. "Better and better, things keep getting better. You just let it happen. It's very exciting." The world of relationships depicted in love-struck fifteen-year-old splendor.

The conversation is so memorable to me, years after Linda's untimely death, because she was not just an older sister. She was like a mother to me, and after searching my memory, I recall no other conversation on relationships with any other family member at any time in my childhood or teenage years.

Her point was clear: relationships just happen. I took it on face value that she was conveying no less than sanctified truths. Beams of ancestral savvy were being passed seamlessly from older sister to younger brother, just as they had been passed from parent to older child previously and before that from my grandparents to parents and so forth until they seemed to originate "back in the day," and this "back in the day" took on a biblical resonance.

Relationships happen.

They don't require work.

For a fifteen-year-old, this can be taken to be an age-appropriate, possibly optimistic view. For an adult, the same perspective signals trouble.

> **Tip:** Begin work on your relationship with the expectation that relationships need work. This approach supports your relationship's potential. Shifting your attitude about what a successful relationship needs—in this way—can help you pull through where you'd otherwise give up.

The two relationship myths at the heart of this chapter are closely related and share the erroneous notion that adult relationships should not take work to maintain:

MYTH #1: RELATIONSHIPS EVOLVE EFFORTLESSLY. Variations of this myth—"If you really loved me, you wouldn't be the way you are, you wouldn't do the things you do"; "I wouldn't have to ask you for what I need, you'd just know"—diminish chances for healing in many relationships. Relationships that might otherwise stand a chance of being worked through wilt and die in the glare of this belief system.

MYTH #2: IF YOU'VE GOT TO "WORK" ON A RELATIONSHIP, IT MEANS THAT THE RELATIONSHIP IS DEFECTIVE. Myth #2 extends logically from myth #1. Myth #2 discourages careful examination of what is going on between you and your partner. This is because noticing that you have a problem, unless you are planning to exit the relationship, is like acknowledging that things have deteriorated beyond the point of repair. *This attitude places thinking about how to work on changing things for the better off-limits.*

CULTURE OF DIVORCE

Images of relationships flash through the media, sparkly attractions to be ogled or envied like prized possessions. Sizzle and glamour masquerade as the glue that binds couples. Meanwhile, expectations related to sustaining relationships dwindle.

If part of your life is a problem, you're not expected to fix it—you're expected to replace it: that's the contemporary mind-set. "Working" on a difficult relationship bucks the current trend of consumeristic thinking. Within this perspective, only problems that can be remedied with a quick fix or replacement, or solved by just saying no or yes, can get legitimate attention.

ADDRESS RESOLVABLE PROBLEMS

The goal in demystifying myths #1 and #2 is to encourage you to attack resolvable problems rather than your relationship itself because problems have arisen that need to be addressed. Working on a relationship while feeling that no work should be necessary if the relationship is worth keeping needs to be understood, in itself, as a personal and cultural problem.

Need to resolve and need to dissolve are not identical.

TRYING TO TRY

Sometimes we are more resistant to the *idea* that our relationship can be worked on than we are to actually working on it. We must, in this sense, do battle with ourselves.

When working with exercises recommended in this book, many partners surprise themselves by their own level of responsiveness to the techniques. Partners often go into the exercises with low expectations, only to become buoyed up when their expectations are exceeded.

Working on problems, even with reluctance, creates possibilities for success. This is why an encouraging atmosphere can make a huge difference and why casual cynicism about one's partner, one's chances for change, or one's relationship can be so harmful.

FEARING CHANGE, CHANGING FEAR

Studies show that significant changes in lifestyle, both positive and negative, are typically upsetting. That's right, *both* positive and negative. Most of us think that when good things happen, we feel great, and any other reaction is strange or weird. However, because significant changes force us out of our secure routines, they compel us to experience degrees of *insecurity*. And insecurity, even if caused by a positive change, doesn't feel good. We try to avoid it if we can. So this finding does make logical sense even though it's not what most of us would have expected the research to show.

Adjusting to new situations—especially, for our purposes, changes in expectations and understanding about important relationships—produces stress, even when making these adjustments results from a *positive* change that we consciously welcome.

Even good change promotes disorientation, *transitional insecurity*. As we change, we sense a gap within ourselves between who we had been and who we are becoming. This transitional juncture can feel like a crisis. Erik Erikson, noted psychoanalyst and developmental theoretician, described the changes in maturational development as a series of crises. The crisis element had to do with whether individuals forded the challenge of each stage of growth and moved on to the next set of challenges or became stranded, arrested in development, without incorporating the necessary skills—meeting the necessary challenges—to move forward. In making changes in our lives, we face the anxiety concerning whether we will be able to integrate the new changes *and* the challenge of understanding who we are as we change. *When we are not yet who we will become yet no longer who we were— who are we?* This is the crux of transitional insecurity.

To the anxiety concerning our new identity as people who have undergone a change, add the discomfort experienced as we sense a *loss* of who we were, and you see how change can induce *terror*— even, as stated above, when the change is positive, expected, and hoped for! Transitions can become misrecognized. Although they constitute integration of the old with the new when they are positive changes, they can be mistaken as representing a generalized deterioration of the core self. Most of us therefore dread personal change, on some level, even though we plan and invite it on other levels. Personal change is a highly conflictual process. Because of this, most of us require support from those around us to succeed. Thinking relationally, the need for changes can be mistaken by partners as a sign that the relationship is losing its stability, falling apart. This is why couples need a lot of support while going through change, even when the process heals their difficulties.

Difficulties people experience in letting go of established patterns in their lives become easily understandable in this light. And the complications couples have in changing their patterns also can be better understood using this logic. We are averse to the loss that change makes inevitable, *even when the change (or modification) involves losing a pattern that has outlived its usefulness.*

KEY QUESTIONS AND INFORMATION

- Do you worry that, even if you were to succeed at making the changes necessary to improve the relationship, these changes would result in disappointment?
- Do you fear that, even before you've tried, results will not be worth the effort?
- These doubts are not a sign that the needed changes cannot be accomplished.
- Do not do yourself the disservice of interpreting these fears to mean that the changes can't be made successfully.
- These doubts are commonly experienced when people undergo relationship distress *and* relationship change.
- These doubts signal the anxiety that the change process produces.
- Understanding these doubts in this way will help you stay focused on accomplishing the positive changes that you and your partner need.

> **Important tip:** Decide whether the exertions required by the change process are worthwhile only after you have made them.

MORE ON TRYING TO TRY

Joan insisted haughtily that she knew herself, that she would not get anything worthwhile from any couples' exercise I might suggest. She said she would not try. End of story? No. Joan had refused to try *in order to* rid herself of the anxiety of investing hope in trying; and in order to sidestep the possibility of becoming vulnerable to yet another disappointment. She felt afraid to risk feeling hopeful about the exercise and, by extension, the work on her relationship. She had been, up to this point, ground down by disappointment. Many partners confront this set of internal obstacles as they begin their work on improving their relationship.

Once she had established that she could make this kind of decision—that is, exert a degree of control over whether she would or would not make herself vulnerable in the couples' work—she felt emboldened to take the risk she initially could not; perhaps she felt she was taking it on her own terms now. Having mobilized herself, she signaled readiness to participate. Her initial refusal to try can be understood as an aspect of her trying to try.

She had mustered needed courage. She had struggled to resist allowing fear and worry to curtail her options; although the struggle was, at most times, invisible to her partner—probably to her as well.

By participating in the exercise even though her stated expectations were low, Joan created an opportunity for herself to differentiate between her *experience* of the exercise and her *expectations* concerning it. In the end, she had successfully battled fears of disappointment and engaged in a process that helped her make needed changes in her idiosyncratic style.

LISTENING FOR EMOTION

Dave later asked her why she had been so negative about trying the exercise at first. She shot back, "I felt hopeless. I guess, when I said it wouldn't help and that I couldn't do it, I was talking about how I felt, not about what I could actually do or not do."

I was impressed with Joan's insight. This confusion—between the attitude she held toward a specific activity and her actual capability to engage in it productively—is common.

Dave was understandably confused. Joan had not deliberately misrepresented herself but was able to only partially represent her convoluted state of mind. After all, it became evident that Joan's prediction—that the exercise couldn't help her—had obscured, not expressed, her internal experience, which included her desire to free herself from feeling overwhelmed by another disappointment. Joan had been unclear about her own state of mind; her feelings had been in flux. This level of complexity in human communication is commonplace, because the nature of communication between people often involves not only diverse elements, but more than one level of consciousness.

Dave wondered how he could have understood what she, herself, was unable to get a handle on. The whole thing seemed so complicated to him.

Understanding and being able to feel what is going on inside one's partner—sometimes called *empathic attunement*—opens doors to the middle ground. Empathic attunement can be verbalized; it also can be a response to what is said by one's partner; but it spans across nonverbal dimensions of communication as well—and the verbal domain is not necessarily the most important.

In situations like Dave's and Joan's, and there are many of these moments in couples' lives, the nonverbal communication, as well as the influence of context, can be used to help them reach mutual understanding. Words, as is clear in the example of Dave's and Joan's confusion, rarely tell the whole story.

A gap between partners' words and their underlying feelings can create difficulties in understanding what they are going through. Problem-solving—rather than fault-finding—ranks high as a valued activity within the middle ground. Love and friendship that evolve over time depend on this spirit.

Food for thought: A dichotomy between words and unacknowledged feelings is not unusual. We, as partners, can
tune into this dimension, anticipate that occasionally we
will face it. When words and actions are not of a piece, we
cannot afford—for the sake of emotional safety in our relationship—to launch into blame mode without first
reflecting on what our partner may be experiencing, which
may not be clear to us at the time.

Responding with self-righteous anger at catching our partner in a
contradiction often destroys possibilities for healing. *Lying, deliberate
deceitfulness, must not be used as a catchall category for understanding confusing or contradictory messages.*

That we are confused does not mean that our partner wishes us to
be. As is discussed skillfully in Douglas Stone, Bruce Patton, and Sheila
Heen's book, *Difficult Conversations*, a sharp distinction must be drawn
between our partner's impact upon us and his or her intention.

Accurate and timely self-expression is a complex skill that takes
practice. For many, it is underdeveloped. Because of lack of skill in
self-expression, confusion between partners can develop. Couples
sometimes fight over issues that result from one or the other partner's
inability to represent a complex state of mind. This type of battle is
patently counterproductive.

To bring dialogue toward the middle ground, Dave—and Joan, for
that matter—must listen to the words spoken and try to grasp feelings
unspoken, or at least anticipate that unspoken feelings may be a part
of the situation at hand. Using hindsight, Dave can think about how
Joan handled this situation, one that was confusing for her. Why
should he bother? Because situations repeat—they frequently come in
patterns. Even should he be unable to figure out *exactly* what she experiences in a given moment, resisting the temptation to jump to conclusions—and blame—is respectful of the inherent richness and complexity of Joan's internal world.

A TIP-OFF

When anxious, many people adopt a manner designed to convince others—and themselves—that they feel in control, because they are not feeling that way and don't want it to become apparent, not even to themselves. The haughty manner with which Joan predicted she had nothing to gain from trying the couples' exercise may be a tip-off for the way she *acts when she is anxious.*

Joan's imperious tone itself may become a signal that Dave can use to identify when she is anxious or confused. Dave may notice that when she is truly confident about what she is predicting—and subsequent experience bears this out—her tone is not imperious but conversational. Dave is learning to listen to more than his partner's words, growing more sensitive to hearing the *feeling* embedded within her words.

"Doesn't this make communication incredibly complicated?" Dave asked me.

My answer to him was that noticing how complicated human communication is doesn't create the complications, just as refusing to notice the complications doesn't make them go away. Not *every* statement or comment requires scrutiny, but to unravel miscommunication, we often need to work at it. Interacting without awareness of these levels of complexity puts partners at a disadvantage.

Although dealing with misunderstanding is not high on the list of favored couples' activities, interpersonal miscues sometimes signal that couples are actively changing meanings in their relationship. Changes do cause confusion. In times of flux, understandings shift—sometimes subtly, sometimes not so subtly. This is not evidence, in itself, that the relationship is destabilizing; it may, in fact, signify productive change is under way.

UNCERTAINTY HAS ITS PLACE

We may feel we understand what our partners have said, but we still hold onto a modicum of uncertainty about what they mean. That's prudent. In general, we tend to react too quickly, defend too vigorously, counterattack too harshly, exit situations without exploring difficulties thoroughly. Proper respect for the complexity of the communication process mitigates against these destructive tendencies.

An element of mystery lies at the heart of communication and at the heart of truth. Albert Einstein said, "The most incomprehensible thing about the world is that it is comprehensible." We need to respect how difficult it is to come to terms with the complexity of our relationship process; at the same time, we need to maintain faith in the fact that, by persevering, we can and will arrive as close to where we wish to be as possible.

As we work within the middle ground, we come to understandings we can rely on. In the midst of a power struggle, however, perceptions are distorted by a need to protect ourselves from our own and, at times, our partner's, fears and anger.

Chapter 10

FERTILE GROUND

Unlike many couples coming in for therapy with communication problems—among other issues—Jean and Lee already shared a middle ground when I met them. What did it look like? Let me recount an anecdote, not a glamorous one, but an example that by virtue of its very ordinariness might be overlooked as an example of middle-ground living.

During a commercial demonstrating a breakthrough in camera technology, Lee announces plans to buy a camera, an expensive one, soon. When Jean suggests postponing the buy, Lee responds testily, "Why do you say that?"

Miffed at Jean's suggestion that he hold up on his purchase, Lee nonetheless manages to listen to her speak about recent bills that have come in. He reconsiders and agrees that waiting makes sense.

Lee had flinched reflexively, momentarily deflated by Jean's remark. Then he was able to shift into an evenhanded regard for what she'd said about their finances. He had enough—not unlimited but *enough*—patience and curiosity to hear her out and consider her point. He took in her perspective. The difference in quality of communication comparing couples who do or do not take this step is monumental.

Many couples converse frequently but have no ongoing dialogue. Dialogue, for our purposes, is a two-sided conversation that helps bring about a meeting of minds and hearts. Too often, conversations involve two people taking turns delivering monologues to one another without listening between turns. Middle ground depends upon listening. Maintaining a balance between accepting your own thoughts and feelings *and* your partner's—this promotes dialogue.

John Gottman, noted researcher on couples, found that he could predict successful relationships, defined in terms of longevity, based on the following crucial element: whether or not women believe their thoughts and feelings have an impact on their partner. The converse also holds: when women feel that their partners neither "get" their point of view nor allow them to affect them—these relationships die.

> **Note:** Gottman's research appears to have been done with heterosexual couples, but the findings, based on my observation and opinion, are applicable to homosexual couples. That is to say, in a partnership where partners feel unable to influence each other, the prognosis for the relationship is poor because their sense of connection will continuously weaken through chronic disappointment.

My observation: in marriages in which husbands allow wives to have impact on them, wives reciprocate in kind. These couples stay together because the trend of mutuality is self-perpetuating. Where partners in a couple allow each other reciprocal impact, a sense of secure attachment grows. Such a couple is tremendously advantaged.

Caveat: impact can be understood as negative in certain situations. For example, the codependent couple affects each other so that making positive change is increasingly difficult. The ways in which these couples influence one another fortifies each other's defenses. Each is blocked from making a difference to the other. Impact without mutuality unravels connection, undermines middle ground.

CODEPENDENCY

Codependency invariably involves one partner, the codependent, assuming responsibility for the needs of the other. The problematic (or addicted) partner whose caretaking needs are claimed by the codependent then relinquishes responsibility for a part of himself—his problematic or addictive behavior—the part of himself with which he experiences great difficulty. The partner with the designated problem (upon whom the other is codependent) then projects responsibility for the addiction onto the codependent partner.

> **Note:** Although the codependent can be tethered to any form of substance abuser—or to individuals with chronic problems that do not involve substances—for the purposes of clarity in the discussion that follows immediately, I will refer to the person with the designated problems as an alcoholic since this is the most common form of addiction.

The concept of codependency was developed in the context of clinical work and pioneering writings in the field of substance abuse. These writings (see Appendix 5) describe the dynamics that maintain a status quo of anguish in the relationship between the alcoholic and her codependent partner. The codependent becomes the keeper of the alcoholic's potential recovery; the alcoholic no longer takes primary responsibility for solving her problems, instead blaming the codependent for not being able to eradicate the problem behavior.

The codependent, in accepting responsibility for the addict's recovery, colludes destructively by perpetuating the illusion that recovery can proceed without the addict demonstrating accountability for her own issues and actions. The codependent enables the addict's continued escape from responsibility by reacting to the addict's self-destructiveness as if it were a signal of the codependent's, and not the addict's, dereliction.

Rather than helping dissipate blame as a focus in the relationship, codependency preserves blame while snuffing out possibilities for dealing with issues more productively. Codependency can be understood as pernicious in that it provides a bogus solution that postpones or evades the enactment of a real one; in this way, it contributes to the perpetuation of behavioral paralysis and stalls recovery.

In such cases, impact does not result in contact but in distance. Denial of the essence of the problem becomes increasingly rooted as the foundation for the relationship. The intensity of impact—the angry scenes that are so typical—functions as a smokescreen to further obscure the necessity for a solution grounded in self-focus and behavioral change. The more enmeshed the codependent is with the alcoholic, the more distanced the alcoholic is from claiming responsibility for recovery and the less well positioned the codependent is from reclaiming a perspective that honors her own authentic self-needs; a vicious, potentially deadly, cycle extends and expands havoc.

Codependent couples who are not involved with an addiction to substances show signs of this pattern as well. Low self-esteem and inability to maintain self-focus in dealing with problems is the underlying hallmark of codependency. The couple for whom self-contempt is projected from one partner to the other and then recirculated so that no one takes responsibility for her own role in the interaction, or claims responsibility for having to *take action* to help break the pattern, also exemplifies codependency. Accusations become a pretext for strengthening the wall of denial for such a pair. This example is taken from clinical practice. Look for the telltale sounds of codependent pseudodialogue:

BONNIE: You're right to treat me like dirt. I'm worthless. But what does that make you for staying with me? You disgust me.

AL: That's good to know. No wonder we fit together so well. Neither or us has a chance of losing anything of value here.

Bonnie takes no responsibility for resolving, healing, or confronting the situation. Her low self-esteem is tethered to her assessment of Al as a loser. Rather than anchoring themselves in a middle ground, they anchor themselves in a black hole of self-revulsion. The more enmeshed with this round robin of insults and put-downs they become, the more distracted they are from a clear vision of what would be needed to help themselves establish a sense of clarity and purpose in their dialogue.

Another classic:

> JOAN: I don't know why I put up with this, but the saddest part is that I have no reason to expect different from you.

> JILL: Do you have any reason to expect different from anyone? You get out what you put in, don't you know.

> JOAN: Did anyone ever tell you that being called inconsiderate is the closest you'll ever come to being called considerate?

> JILL: No. It's so kind and considerate of you to give me a heads-up about that. Maybe that's why I stay with you—you're always teaching me new and wonderful things about myself.

Despite the sarcasm and put-downs, Jill and Joan had genuine affection for each other and, in many ways, represented each other's main connection to a sense of family. Even with their bitterness, much was accomplished with Jill and Joan after they could change the pattern of hurling a continuous barrage of sarcastic abuse at each other. Practicing many of the basic guidelines for dialogue and related exercises helped them develop an awareness of their patterns and make changes.

UNPACKING IMPACT FURTHER

Collaborative communication represents the fruit of a perspective that features mutual acknowledgment, the hallmark of the middle ground.

In the middle ground, the feeling "What am I doing here, talking to myself?" does not reign supreme. Embedded in the relational process that results in a person having impact on her partner is the notion that the partner has *listened* to what the other has said, and he has *taken it seriously* enough to integrate it into his thoughts and behavior. In such a relationship, partners act in response to having taken in one another's communication, rather than simply reacting to the other's message by pushing it away, that is to say, defending against it.

LEE AND THE MIDDLE GROUND

What is Lee's stance in listening to and taking in Jean's contribution to the dialogue about spending? Lee does not "give in" but "participates in" the relationship by accommodating.

Although like-mindedness per se is not a goal in creating a relational middle ground, points of honest agreement emerge more frequently and spontaneously in a nonadversarial atmosphere.

By not purchasing his camera at this time—*because* he has open-mindedly considered Jean's perspective—Lee affirms that he thinks she is "on his team." His actions speak this. He does not respond contentiously to her remark simply because it does not agree with his own perspective. He allows her influence on him. Her ability to convey her information in a manner that invites him to do so is as significant a contribution. They work together.

OTHER MIDDLE-GROUND QUALITIES?

Acknowledgment of each other's contributions to the relationship, not always explicit, characterizes middle-ground interaction. The middle ground functions as an area of the relationship in which partners validate personal qualities they appreciate in each other.

Where a functional middle ground flourishes, nurturing often occurs indirectly. For example, Jean is someone who sometimes has problems taking her ideas seriously. Lee's middle-ground responses in the example above strengthen Jean's belief in herself. Lee and Jean accomplish this without bringing explicit attention to issues such as building self-confidence. Middle-ground relating engenders a well-spring of these benefits.

Jean and Lee are able to balance a sense of their individuality with a sense of their togetherness; the one does not muscle out the other. Neither feels alone, and neither feels that, apart from their mate, they have no life of their own.

BALANCED IN THE MIDDLE

Let's examine two scenarios that bring to light some aspects of non-defensive communication in the middle ground that can make the difference between functioning as allies or as adversaries.

Scenario #1: While watching television, Jean sings along with the performer on the screen. Lee wisecracks, "Please don't think about leaving your day job." Jean understands Lee's joke as playful attention directed at her. She finds this entertaining, not oppressive. Lee sees from Jean's response that a reserve of goodwill has been established between them. Jean trades barbs with Lee to bring home this point: "That was cute. Not that funny, but cute. You're lucky your stock is so high with me, or else," in a mock-threat of retaliation.

Scenario #2: On another day, on which Jean has had an unsettling experience prior to coming home, she sees red when Lee pokes fun at her. Lee delivers what would ordinarily pass as playful sarcasm, and Jean takes offense.

Where is the middle ground to be discovered here? Is it relevant only when people feel good? Who is available for what is a key element in considering how a middle-ground moment gets constructed?

Even with all the positive understandings in their relationship, Jean, given a heightened state of vulnerability, responds differently than she would otherwise. Who doesn't?

WHO'S IT ALL ABOUT?

If Lee interprets Jean's response as a message to him about himself rather than a statement from her about herself, it'll be more difficult to reconnect.

Lee responds nondefensively in this second scenario. He points out that Jean's response to his joke is not what he had expected. He cues her into this perception by saying, without reproach, "I was only joking, honey. Is something bothering you?" Up to this point, Jean had been unaware that she was feeling different than usual. Lee's remark is instructive.

In the middle ground, partners make use of each other; they take each other in and, sometimes even when angry, can work with the possibility that understandings can be reached.

Jean thinks, "Things may feel tense between us at this moment, but we aren't enemies." It may not be the only thing she's thinking, but something serves to put a brake on her anger. Her anger flashes quickly when she's tense, but she does not allow it to escalate into a destructive tantrum, particularly since Lee has offered her a point of connection.

BLIND SPOT

Outside the middle ground, the meaning of events typically becomes fixed for one or both members of the couple. What is understood is felt to be understood conclusively; *reflection on what is understood does not occur.* The glass is deemed half full or half empty, period, full stop. This mind-set leaves little room to forge a middle ground.

For instance, when Jean told Lee to delay getting his camera, for a flash he experienced what Jean said as an attempt to exert power over him. If he had been able to articulate the flash of feeling, he would have sounded like this: "What's going on here? I'm talking about me and what I want to do. Why do you have to get into this? Can't I simply do what I want sometimes without feeling that I have to run it past you? Is the issue really budget, or is it that you have a need to control me?"

If they were a couple with no middle ground, typically, no matter what else was said, Lee's mind would remain made up on the belief that Jean's need to control him was the only relevant factor. No room for dialogue.

Lee's flexibility in considering other ways of understanding the event—Jean's intervening on his fantasy of getting the camera soon— opens up a middle ground so the issue is not relegated, by default, to the realm of a power struggle.

MIDDLE-GROUND THINKING

Holding in mind this understanding—that events can be perceived in more than one way depending on the perspective from which they are experienced—leaves open room for awareness that no matter how clearly we see or think we see a situation, our perspective *may* be marred by a blind spot. My walk with Julie is an example of an experience I had with my own blind spot.

When Jean came home (in scenario 2) after having experienced something unsettling, she was unaware that the experience had affected her mood. She was out of touch with herself emotionally— had a blind spot in her emotional awareness—and Lee perceived it. He did not impose this perception on her but explored it with her by showing concern about her mood.

Our partners may have clear access to the very spot that we can't see. In a middle-ground situation, their ability to see something we can't, or don't, doesn't mean they are outdoing us, competing against us, or undermining our perspective; if we can think about them as adding to it, we are greatly advantaged. Our partner's ability to offer us something we haven't thought of or seen ourselves is a gift, part of the bounty of the relationship. When are two heads better than one? When they are allied. How are two heads better than one? Allied.

MINIEXERCISE

Can you recall the last disagreement that you had with your partner? How open were you to the possibility that what he or she had to say, even if it didn't mirror what you had been thinking, might be useful or helpful to you? If you can answer this question with a yes, you have a trend of strength to develop further in your relationship. If the answer is no, target this as an area that may need work.

TRADITIONAL BLIND SPOTS

I'd like to give two examples of traditional blind spots.

You are driving on the interstate with your partner, and a vehicle approaches quickly on your rear right on a diagonal fifteen feet back. Your partner realizes that more than likely, because of the placement of the oncoming vehicle, you don't see it. Your partner senses your blind spot and informs you of the situation. If your relationship is such that this teamwork is inhibited, much of the richness of working together is either underdeveloped or has eroded. A breach in communication such as this creates a lack of safety in the relationship.

Second example: You and your partner prepare to attend an event that may open professional opportunities for you. You've put energy into presenting yourself as appropriately and fastidiously as possible.

Your partner notices a stain on the rear of your shirt where it would be difficult for you to see. Blind spot, as in the first example, is literal, not metaphorical. Obviously, most people would wish their partner to tell them what they'd seen.

Translating this concept into the emotional realm is not always so clear cut. When Jean came home, she was indeed in what she would acknowledge was a bad mood. But as is not unusual, she was unaware of how much it was coloring her responses. She had slipped into feeling somewhat down and didn't want to burden Lee by talking about what had happened with her colleague at work—the source of her upset. She felt she had been mistreated but anticipated that Lee would not be sympathetic, *because of her mood*. Jean felt she had not handled the situation well and was not particularly sympathetic to her own side of the experience; it was hard for her to imagine anyone else, even Lee, being supportive.

When Lee brings her attention to his perception that something seemed to be bothering her, Jean responds nondefensively and allows him to help her focus on what is going on with her at the time. Had Lee not had the social skill to point this out in a way that Jean could hear, if he, without intending to shame her, had a reproachful or possibly even a neutral tone, Jean might not have been able to open up (to herself or Lee) and felt even more isolated; Jean needed to hear a sympathetic tone to risk opening up. Much of the meaning of comments like Lee's gets conveyed through tone of voice and body language. The words are only one—as discussed above—and usually *not* the most important aspect of one's interpersonal communication.

Most people would like their mate to mention if they notice a stain on their shirt or a car approaching irregularly on the highway. I am not advocating "back seat" (or "passenger seat") driving here but saying that, in many situations, an open flow of information can prevent danger.

Do most people want their partner to tell them if they notice that—emotionally—something strikes them as amiss? Such comments, framed and accepted as support, exemplify the middle-ground dialogue.

Sustaining middle-ground communication in any area of the relationship infuses other areas with possibilities for breakthrough. Having no middle ground to return to means being with a partner who cannot contribute to your cause—cannot tell you that you have a stain on your shirt when it's something you need to know, cannot tell you when you're being unresponsive or acting angrily when it's something it would benefit you to know. If a couple can't create a middle ground when confronting an issue like the appreciation of casual humor—as Lee and Jean do—think of how difficult working out miscommunication in the sexual or financial arena can be.

FLEXIBILITY BUILDS TRUST

In the first scenario, Lee jokes. In the second scenario, when things are not going as well at first, Lee jokes again. What goes on in the latter—the quality of Lee's response to Jean when she is not available as an audience for his humor—tells her that he does not take her feelings for granted. Her emotional state, not her being a foil for his humor, is his abiding concern. His flexibility in the matter conveys this. She has been reassured and taken care of without having asked him to do either.

SENSITIVITY TO MOOD

By noticing and articulating his question, about whether anything is bothering her, Lee prompts her to include what she is feeling in their dialogue. He touches on her mood and, in that respect, inhabits it with her. It is no longer foreign to him. She is no longer alone in it.

Relational building blocks are fashioned in moments; moments of connection can be restorative or foundational or both. These form the live core of a loving relationship. Lee's comment shows his availability to help Jean contain a difficult feeling. This restores connection.

IT TAKES TWO

Lee cannot take sole credit for bringing on this connection. Jean takes his implicit offer of connection and, by responding in kind, makes it what it becomes—a joining within the middle ground. Were she to miss—misinterpret, misconstrue, misapprehend—then they would both miss together. Regardless of external appearance, middle-ground experience necessarily involves *both* partners' active participation.

EXERCISE: COMPARE-AND-CONTRAST WORKSHEET

1. Lee initially felt like arguing with Jean but then was able to make a shift. Can you identify with making this kind of shift in a situation that you face with your partner? Please describe it below. If you cannot imagine this, describe what would interfere with your making a shift.

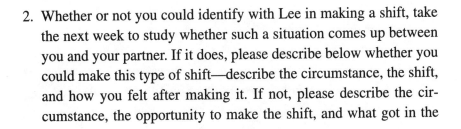

2. Whether or not you could identify with Lee in making a shift, take the next week to study whether such a situation comes up between you and your partner. If it does, please describe below whether you could make this type of shift—describe the circumstance, the shift, and how you felt after making it. If not, please describe the circumstance, the opportunity to make the shift, and what got in the

way of making this shift. Either way—whether you are enhancing your awareness of how to shift or the obstacles to making it—this study can help you integrate and practice these important middle-ground concepts.

_____

_____

_____

_____

_____

_____

_____

3. Consider for a moment whether you feel that you have any "blind spots," that is, areas where you tend to overestimate or underestimate a situation, areas where you tend to, with hindsight, realize that you have a pattern of misunderstanding. If you can identify such a blind spot, describe it below.

_____

_____

_____

_____

_____

_____

_____

4. Consider for a moment whether your partner has any blind spots. If so, how do you relate to them? Do you tend to be critical? Do you feel you are helpful and supportive in helping your partner deal with what you consider to be blind spots? Do you relate to your partner with respect or contempt? After all, in this situation, you

may have knowledge that your partner lacks. Do you help him or her acquire that knowledge, or do you shame your partner for not having it? Please describe the blind spot, if you can, and your responses to it. (Note: Most partners feel vulnerable in relation to their blind spots.)

_____

_____

_____

_____

_____

_____

_____

5. If you have identified a blind spot in your partner and interacted with your partner about it, please describe your partner's response to your approach to his or her blind spot.

_____

_____

_____

_____

_____

_____

_____

_____

Chapter 11

ROUNDING OUT
THE MIDDLE GROUND—
FINAL REMARKS

Most Thursdays, in the early afternoon, at the Institute for Contemporary Psychotherapy in Manhattan, a group of family and couples' therapists—I am one of them—sit around a large table and talk shop. I look forward to these meetings for the camaraderie and for the opportunity to hear others' ideas and feelings about what works or doesn't work in their couples' therapy practice.

At a certain point, as the ideas about the middle ground were becoming clearer to me, I began to listen differently to my colleagues' presentations. I'd hear them set the stage for their clients to resolve problems. I'd hear them help clarify confusions and challenge their clients to make needed adjustments. I could picture the effective, sometimes inspired, couples' work they were engaged in. Yet I felt that *something* in their cogent narratives was either missing or had been skipped over. I came to realize that the concept of the middle ground had worked its way into my consciousness to the extent that it was becoming hard for me to conceptualize couples' work without reference to it. In my thinking, I'd insert it into the work I was hearing about, and it always made an elegant fit. The middle-ground ideas, it seemed to me, offered a further level of clarification, a further explication of how and why couples were getting better when they were, or a way of seeing that something essential in their relationship had not cohered yet. These moments were precursors to the day, now a long way behind, when I began to hear myself say out loud to my clients, "I'm going to teach you about an idea called the middle ground and how it can help you work through the difficulties that you're facing as a couple." And then I began to share my ideas about the middle ground with colleagues and to get feedback and support.

I began using middle-ground concepts to help me pinpoint moments of connection and of disconnection that I perceived in my clients' communications with each other. In this way, I began to forge a nontechnical *common* language for our discussions. This talk strengthened the therapeutic alliance between my clients and myself by letting them in on my thoughts concerning key aspects of the real action—including tactics and strategies—of the healing process.

Other therapeutic advantages to the language of the middle ground intrigued me. Unlike other metaphors for relationships that therapists use—such as a plant, a house, a boat, and so on—the middle ground is not tied to a specific visual image but can conveniently shift shape to serve diverse aspects of the work. For example, the middle ground evokes a space that can appear, disappear, and reappear, just as key issues do. You can see the middle ground as a growing thing—like a garden—but also liken it to a tool that facilitates needed work, to a divining rod that helps locate hidden resources, to a well that provides a vital replenishment, to a stepping stone that makes crossing rough patches feasible, to an oasis that motivates the search for greener pastures, to a sanctuary that affords the promise of peace and opportunities for respite and reflection, like a proverbial bridge over troubled water, like a tunnel that plows beneath dangers and disruptions and moves its travelers forward. Where can a couple cool down anger? Where can a couple warm their connection after a bitter exchange? The middle ground provides a composite of images and ideas that are available for use as needed. The middle ground can serve as a compass that points couples to what is doable. It can also help couples discriminate between aspects of their relationship they need to allow to fade and those they need to renew.

When a couple seeks clarity in formulating their next (immediate) objective, clear and useful images do not always present themselves. This can be anticipated and is not a cause for worry. This is evidence of the stop-and-go syncopated rhythm of couples' work. Though the image concerning what is needed has not formed, this does not mean that it will not form. Although the middle ground is not a crystal ball, it is a place in which just such images develop. With the help of the most subtle of tinctures—acceptance, memory, dream, reflection, patience, love—a middle-ground picture takes shape and reveals direction.

PARADOX AND THE MIDDLE GROUND

The middle ground represents the hope that is so often embedded in bitter hopelessness, as well as the power that many who feel helpless unknowingly possess. The element of paradox is stamped into the design of every middle-ground molecule. Hope within hopelessness, power within powerlessness—the middle ground calls attention, by its very structure, to the contradictory elements inherent in the processes of growth and change—blossoms of the new foreshadow obsolescence of the old. For example, starting from a place where you acknowledge feeling stuck, by adopting a middle-ground perspective, you reflect upon this "stuckness." As a result, your relationship to this stuckness becomes altered—the stuckness is no longer something you can do nothing about. Being able to think about it helps you generate new ideas about it, perhaps one that helps you do something you previously felt unable to, or you may come to a realization, depending on the issue, that you need help in dealing with the problem. This shift may convert stuckness to a feeling that you are moving toward a solution; in other words, the inertia of being stuck can be upended in this way. At this point, you've moved from feeling-stuck-and-held-fast-to-one-spot, which equates to hopelessness, to feeling-stuck-the-hold-upon-you-loosened—the promise of new momentum forward makes a difference. The middle-ground perspective has allowed you to open up a crack between feeling stuck forever and feeling stuck temporarily. The *dialectic* between these opens up to create all kinds of possibilities for further movement. You take a dead-end feeling and examine it carefully from all angles until you find a way to see it as being not quite as overwhelming as you had imagined, even if the thought that leads to this conclusion is something like, "Well, this being so difficult doesn't mean I'm pinned under it indefinitely, but I may need some help dealing with it"—that's a legitimate and productive response to feeling trapped, and it is always an option! Having created this *dialectical* perspective in regard to stuckness often works to replace the rigidity that held stuckness in place. Without the dialectic, stuck means stuck; it means you can't move. With the dialectic, stuck can mean stuck and can't move *or* stuck and can't move right now, but there is a possibility that things will change. Such a small difference makes a huge difference, if you see what I mean.

Case illustration: Remember Rob and Mark, the gay couple discussed in chapter 3? They were socially isolated and had no friends who were couples, and this hurt their ability to identify themselves as a couple. They had grown accustomed to thinking that this was simply the way they would have to be if they were to remain together—isolated. They viewed the issue as a dead end, saying, "If we haven't done it yet, it ain't gonna get done." I raised the issue anyway and suggested that they attend a meeting at the Center—a gay, lesbian, transgender community center—located in downtown Manhattan. I encouraged them to give it a try since, from their perspective, they had nothing to lose; they already had nothing in the socializing-as-a-couple department, and if things went as poorly as they expected, so what? This approach wouldn't work with everybody, but I had a feeling it would persuade them to take a chance, and it did. And so the status of the issue at hand began to turn from being a *dead end* to being an issue susceptible to possible improvement—although they saw this possibility as extremely slim. Their eventual connection to the Center yielded social contact that greatly reduced their sense of isolation as a couple. They went from stuck to unstuck by virtue of their willingness to engage in a conversation that, from their point of view, would probably not be of any use to them. Their willingness to entertain the discussion, consider the suggestion, and explore its possibilities nudged the issue from where it had been into the middle ground.

By the way, another important aspect of middle-ground connection, not mentioned elsewhere in this book, is that it often spurs connection between couples and their community. Once a feeling of emotional isolation is relieved within a relationship, couples need support from and connection to the larger community to sustain the gains they have made together. Or for another way of looking at the issue, in order to safeguard and make possible relief from isolation within a couple's relationship, connection to the larger community—where this is lacking—can be extremely helpful, sometimes crucial to spurring improvement in the couple's relationship. The middle-ground approach, in this sense, serves as a connection point within *and* beyond the couple.

Human growth inevitably involves paradoxical elements. Growth involves change, and as we change, we no longer remain who we were. So how do we remain consistent with the person who wanted to make changes if, by changing, we become other than the person we were? Is the person we become still essentially the person who we had been or essentially someone different? As discussed earlier, these are some reasons that change can be scary. Middle-ground thinking—thinking rooted in consideration of the relation between what is and what can be—helps partners anticipate the paradoxes inherent in the change process.

Henri Bergson, Nobel Prize–winning French philosopher, provides a lovely example of this change paradox in an essay from *Creative Evolution*. He describes a man stranded on the bank of a body of water who sees, on the opposite shore, his path continuing. The man is stuck. He has no boat and cannot swim, so he will have to discontinue his journey. Right? Of course not. He wades in, flails his arms and legs, and arrives at the other side. By the time he gets to the other side, he is the same man, of course, but he is no longer a nonswimmer. People are capable of many kinds of changes. How can a nonswimmer get across a body of water? By exercising creativity. How can a couple get past an obstacle that seems—in the way they define their capabilities—to be insurmountable? Most often they get across by learning to do something they thought they couldn't do, by summoning their creativity and a spirit of optimism that allows them to imagine the possibility of achieving their objective. The nonswimmer needed to imagine he might make it across; otherwise, his flailing would be too dispirited to get him across. Many couples, feeling the weight of repeated disappointments, feel stuck on the shore of unhappiness, unable to proceed to where their path resumes. By purchasing a book like this, seeing a therapist, or both, people—despite all reservations and doubts—find themselves wading into the water. In the process, many learn that being stuck where they are or going under do not constitute their only options; a third option emerges. The two options that most couples readily acknowledge are these: accept the situation just as it is or reject it entirely. *This third option, working with the situation creatively, is the basis upon which the middle ground is organized.* Every swimmer was once a nonswimmer.

As discussed earlier, Amanda could not separate the anger that Carl felt as a result of unresolved anger in his relationship with his family from her expectation that, in relationships, she would forever be paired with a man who would find fault with her and rain anger on her. She believed she would never be able to get past this juncture. She believed herself stuck. When it came to men, she was a nonswimmer —she would never escape this shore on which they railed at her. By daring to suspend this long-held belief about the nature of her relationships with men—and with Carl in particular—she listened to Carl's discussion of how things had been between himself and his parents differently than before. Although the plot lines were familiar to Amanda, she now could connect to *his* feelings and put herself in his place. She allowed herself to take in new information about how he formed and who he was. She may have been a nonswimmer up to this point, but she was learning to listen like a swimmer; she was getting unstuck. She came to the conclusion that much of Carl's anger had nothing to do with her. To produce this thought required a shift in perspective. This shift became an important step into the middle ground for them both—she was now buoyant on the water.

POWER STRUGGLES AND BOUNDARIES

Couples who occupy Square One almost invariably square off into power struggles. The middle-ground concept offers a well-suited corrective to this power-struggle predicament. Because the idea of the middle ground throws partners' attempts to control the other into high relief, transgressions become increasingly visible and, as a result, more possible to talk about and prevent. Efforts of either partner to control the other *eviscerate* the middle ground, which ceases to function if either partner violates this precept. Certain behaviors—two quick examples of this are bullying and stonewalling—clearly have no place in a middle-ground process, unless it is to communicate about them for the purpose of reducing and/or eliminating them. Use of the middle-ground framework telegraphs this message.

The middle ground, then, stands in as a set of explicit boundaries (guidelines) that can help rule out destructive behaviors and attitudes. This is one of the ways in which it fosters emotional safety. If partners understand this aspect of the middle ground, they have grasped a lot about how they need to contribute to their work on their relationship— and they don't need a PhD in clinical psychology to *get* it. The middle-ground language helps them feel like insiders in their process of renewal and supports them in feeling they either have, or have the opportunity to regain, greater control over their life situation.

WHAT'S NEXT? OR: ARE WE THERE YET?

Couples ask, "What can I do now to move myself and our relationship toward or further into the middle ground?" This question is always pertinent for partners. Work with the middle ground poses this immediate and unremitting challenge. The concept explicitly demands work on workable problems. The middle-ground ethos includes the idea that *something* useful can always be done, in terms of couples' work, and that the work be considered in—that is, broken down into—doable units, which are cast in immediate relational terms. By this I mean that to figure out what to do next, you've got to consult how you feel and who you are, as well as who your partner is and what he or she has expressed. Working in the middle ground means you constantly coordinate feelings and actions in creating connection in the here and now. If I am angry, for example, and I ask myself: "What do I need to do next to take what is going on between me and my partner closer to, or directly into, the middle ground?" I may realize that simply trying to think about the next step separates me from habitual reactive behavior and that this, in itself, turns me toward the middle ground. Then the question becomes, "What next? What can take me further? What can take 'us' further?"

To move in a productive direction, partners must think in a focused manner of the immediate needs of the moment and of the defining characteristics of the larger moment they share in their life with their partner.

Middle-ground thinking involves integrating what you need to do, who you are, who your partner is, and what your partner needs to do; these are all inextricably linked. In other words, you've always got to be taking each other into account.

Working within the middle ground requires that you and your partner continue getting to know each other better and better.

USER-FRIENDLY MIDDLE GROUND

Occasionally, after having used the term *middle ground* sparingly myself, I hear clients refer to it in a context that makes clear that they grasp the gist of what I had meant. Some ask questions about what I mean by the middle ground. Does it mean the work is geared toward compromise? What am I supposed to do with blaming thoughts and accusations if the idea is to work toward *not blaming* and *not accusing*? Many questions arise and lead toward discussion concerning the structure of the couples' work and what makes for productive communication.

Dysfunctional communication patterns that wall partners off from each other are common in a couples' therapy practice. For partners who feel stuck to imagine the wall between them as a potential connecting piece (they might imagine a wall with the potential to support a door or window or both), they need to have a way to talk about how they can work cooperatively to modify the structure of their lives together, using craft and ingenuity—heart, reason, and imagination—rather than resorting to tactics of despair and destruction. The stuff of these walls is alive—each partner supplies respective defenses composed of thoughts and feelings; therefore, these walls cannot be dynamited. Tools—considered ways of approaching the creation of opportunities for meaningful human contact—have to be handled with adequate know-how so that the living material is not destroyed in remodeling. The middle ground affords a safe place to practice attaining just such know-how.

DELIBERATION

An atmosphere of *deliberation* is needed for couples' work to flow. The term *emotional safety* is a key aspect of what makes deliberation possible. It has an abstract feeling to many partners, yet within the middle-ground realm its appearance is dynamic. Emotional safety is not a bland phenomenon; it signifies strength and a resolve, a determination to protect and respect boundaries and standards of mutual care and concern. Reflection and patience—two other important ideas that, if they ever had any, have lost considerable sex appeal over the years—gain by a middle-ground makeover; each entails a degree of savvy that makes everyday living flow. Life without reflection and patience can easily turn deadly. In light of all the syndromes and addictions that leave individuals battered by and submissive to their own impulsivity, the formulation "Life without reflection and patience can easily turn deadly" seems to fit our times like a pair of skin-tight jeans.

The terms *reflection* and *patience*—words not ordinarily found in the flash-focused lexicon of commercial advertising—are redeemed as powerhouse workhorses within the middle-ground perspective. These central notions—along with such other touch points as the "negative attention span" and the "dark-adapted eye," to name a couple—impose a frame of reference that signals readiness to work on problems in a certain spirit.

Grasping what that spirit is about itself becomes therapeutic for partners who are despairing and angry, because the spirit of the middle ground is unflinchingly and unapologetically optimistic. It is a spirit of connection and open possibilities, an invitation to take a bold and thorough inventory of your feelings and thoughts and sift through the negative to find the positive within. Please consider this: Anger contains disappointment, which contains hopes dashed, which contain love waiting to be affirmed and then moved (perhaps moved back) into a central place in a couple's life. Like opening up a series of Russian nesting dolls, one inside the other inside the other, getting back to the true potential of the relationship is a matter of handling the emotional material with care, compassion, and curiosity.

In relationships conducted in an atmosphere of hostility, the very discussion of the middle ground can invite truce—not simply a cessation of warfare, but an agreement to a set of understandings that advantage the prospect of leaving the state-of-siege mentality for good.

We Americans preoccupy ourselves with the sizzle and glamour of the media, the stock market, fashion, material allure. To bring us into a sense of connection with our deeper selves, our deeper abilities to love, our deeper connection with our partnership as part of a couple, we need to explore how the relationship we seek to renew and enjoy joins to our more general partnership with community and then to our universal partnership with Life itself. We must make deliberate efforts to forge these bonds between our lives and the lives around us and to Life itself, or we suffer feeling isolated. Our culture emphasizes what is consumable, not what is lasting. If we wish our commitment and our partner's commitment to be large and deep, they must be grounded in something large and deep, something unconditional. We, as humans, are certainly a significant aspect of Life, but by no means the only one. Love in isolation ultimately creates circumstances of isolation, which are not conducive to love. Love that accepts connection and is conducted in the spirit of connection can not only thrive but renews itself continuously.

Establishing a middle-ground connection allows partners to go from feeling alone together to embracing togetherness. Often, couples' work involves tackling issues that may *seem* to have been settled but turn out to have been buried. Old pains are revisited and reapproached in a spirit of compassion and with the intent of helping partners feel relieved, understood, and unburdened so that they can make a new beginning. For example, recall Roy and Mira's experience. Roy's failure to take Mira's feelings seriously was a chronic issue that lay buried within the foundation of their relationship. Prior to therapy, the couple had been unable to raise and deal with it effectively. When Roy finally *got* the fact that his continuing refusal to take Mira's feelings seriously was edging him onto the verge of ending their relationship, he could look back and reevaluate his position—not only in the moment, but throughout their relationship. In addition, he could take himself seriously enough to see that the consequences of his actions were going to be painful and considerable unless he allowed himself to *take Mira's feelings to heart*. He plunged in, and a new chapter in their life began.

This new chapter that ensues when partners can repave a path to each other's hearts and minds is the crux of how middle-ground break-throughs develop. Partners find each other after having become lost and detached from the love they had shared. A house marked with pain hidden within the convoluted folds of a deteriorating relationship issues forth little but sadness, or the anger that masks the same. When work in the middle ground clears out the muck and replaces misunderstanding and disconnection with touches of renewal, it is not only *feelings* that lighten; a spirit of breakthrough soars as well. Of course, identifying, modulating, articulating, processing, and coming to terms with feelings—all this is central to relational renewal. But on a more basic level, partners can be said to *refind* each other and to claim, or reclaim, the feeling and the spirit of love, which, in so many resplendent ways, resonates with the spirit of the middle ground.

APPENDIX 1

APPROACHING COUPLES' WORK

For many couples, healing relationship difficulties requires the help of a therapist. Recognizing this need when it exists is a genuine strength. Making skillful use of help signals creativity, maturity, and resourcefulness. Stubborn clinging to a posture that disallows reaching out to others often indicates pseudo-self-sufficiency—an underlying dependency wedded to emotional paralysis.

How do most couples approach couples' work? What does it feel like? In this section, I'll address these and related questions. I will also discuss my own stance, objectives, and aspects of my perspective as a couples' therapist.

STARTING

Most frequently, couples coming in for couples' therapy report "communication problems" as their primary concern.

THERAPIST: What brings you in for therapy at this time?

PARTNER #1: We don't communicate.

PARTNER #2: That's right. We're having problems with communication.

This could mean a conflict over child rearing or one of the countless variations of breakdowns in trust. He just doesn't get it. She just doesn't get it. There may be feelings of betrayal, of being taken for granted, of being unappreciated. Conflicts of interest over whether or when to have children are a common problem. Jealousies and assorted conflicts relating to a third party are often what spark an approach to couples' therapy. Some couples cannot come to terms with the way one or the other partner responded to a pregnancy or a miscarriage. A backlog of bad feelings connected to in-laws can cause tribulations. Sometimes each partner comes armed with a detailed accounting of the other's relational failings and declares that moving forward will not be possible until all accounts are rectified. And then other couples simply want things to be justified. There may be a resistance on someone's part to making a definitive commitment. And there may be a resistance to accepting a commitment as definitive no matter how emphatically it is given. There may be unresolved feelings about an abortion. Problems due to emotional or physical violence, an atmosphere of intimidation, emotional blackmail, disparity in desire for sex—these are other reasons that commonly bring people in for couples' therapy. Problems with substance abuse are so prevalent that this problem must be explored routinely. Infidelity can end a relationship or begin the rebuilding of one. Nonsexual triangles that threaten the relationship must be explored. Social isolation or too much socializing outside the primary relationship can affect a couple's sense of connection. Too much or too little involvement with family of origin can be problematic. Money problems come in all denominations and often create bankruptcies in trust as well as capital. Cross-cultural confusions are not uncommon. The list billows on and on.

Many couples lack confidence about the couples' work making a difference. They look toward the work with a jaundiced or, what I describe earlier as, a *dark-adapted eye*. Often people think that *they* personally might be able to benefit from the therapy but have grave doubts about whether the same can be said for that other who is being dragged along. It's unusual for both partners to be equally motivated at the beginning of therapy.

Many times, one comes in thinking: *If he were capable of working this thing out, we wouldn't be here. We'd have worked it out already. I'm not sure why we're here. What can be accomplished?*

Of the partners who come in with the conviction that their partner is the heart of the problem and not capable of making necessary changes, some percentage are right. Couples' therapy can be used as a way to gauge whether partners are committed to trying to repair the damage in the relationship. These couples may find, in their couples' therapy work, a way to clarify their need to separate.

Other couples come in thinking, feeling, and sometimes saying that their situation is hopeless. Only *these* couples are voicing fear of disappointment and lack of confidence in being able to make something positive happen. Often they feel they have no clue how to proceed. A critical dimension in the relationship is missing, and they can neither identify it nor envision a way to create it. These couples want and need to create a middle ground—only they have no idea how to start.

Restraining the tendency to blame your partner for all the difficulties in the relationship is one key starting point. If you can accomplish this, there is good reason to believe that you will find yourself able to invite a "new beginning" in which the tone of how you relate supports and nurtures hope for a better life together.

For couples whose relationship is fragile and painful, this step—releasing blame and focusing on making positive changes—has huge positive implications. If your relationship has been stalled on the "blame" plateau, you can regain direction, but you will need perseverance. Perseverance maximizes possibilities for a successful outcome. Without perseverance, the relationship potential that I described earlier will, more than likely, go unrealized.

If you are one of those, decidedly in the minority, who take all the blame for what is wrong in the relationship on yourself, this is a habit of thought that you'll need to scrutinize. You are willing to take responsibility for your actions, which is a terrific starting point, but insistence on taking *all* the blame *may* stem from poor self-esteem. Identifying areas that need improvement is important, but recognizing and working with strengths is important as well.

IMPOSSIBLENESS

Laurie thinks: *This therapist comes recommended. If he's half as good as my friend Sarah says, then he should see right away that Jack is what's wrong with the relationship. I'm looking for him to take some information and then let Jack have it. He'll be able to do it in a way that I never could. He may ask me to sit outside in the waiting room while he does what he needs to do. I'll rejoin when Jack's impossibleness has been fixed.*

Laurie's position, deliberately caricatured here, is not unusual. On coming to couples' therapy, each partner, more often than not, nurses hope that the therapist will identify their partner as the cause of all difficulties.

Jack may be thinking: *I hope this guy knows what he's doing. A marriage license is not license to complain 24/7. Once he draws a bead on what I'm up against here, he'll put a stop to it. Maybe there'll be some things I can work on too, but honestly, I don't know what they would be.*

FIRST OBJECTIVES

Jack and Laurie, as many couples do, enter therapy with a state of siege mentality. My first objective will be to help them establish a sense of emotional safety together. Setting up guidelines for dialogue will be part of this. (See chapter 7 for explicit guidelines). Helping Jack and Laurie talk to each other without automatically getting defensive or angry will open possibilities that they will listen to each other.

The language of the middle ground provides an intuitive way to talk about the healing process. This enables attachment to become richer and deeper.

These objectives take a good deal of work to accomplish. Learning to speak without blaming takes time once this has become an ingrained habit. (See the Basic Three-Step Exercise.)

MY STANCE

I ally myself with both partners as equally as possible. I do my best to help both partners create middle ground. I do not take sides. Sometimes it's hard not to, depending on what's going on.

However, I do take sides against abuse, against using problems in the relationship to enable substance abuse or abuse of any kind. If abuse is a problem in your relationship, be sure to read Appendix 4.

If I spend more time with one partner than the other, I'll try to balance the experience over the course of working together. I want to understand what is going on from each partner's viewpoint and compare that with what seems to be in their own best interests and in the interests of their relationship. Part of my job is to help each to articulate their point of view, to "find their voice" and to understand their partner's.

Appendix 2
ENVISIONING POSSIBILITIES

I f you remain committed to the "old" way—the power struggle, the blaming, the anger—you miss opportunities for healing as they present themselves.

By heeding signs, you can make the important changes you need; the turns, once so elusive, can be anticipated. In this book, I clarify which signals you need to look for, to listen for, to tune into. When you're steering on automatic pilot, with a sense of direction based on failed experience, healing directions elude you.

In the middle ground, your observation and imagination combine. Your resolve and compassion can be accessed. Understanding grows.

GUIDED VISUALIZATION SCRIPTS

I use this warmup exercise as an opening section for each of the visualization exercises that follow.

To get the most benefit from the guided visualization exercises, I recommend that you either (1) have someone read the warmup and an accompanying script to you or (2) read the warmup and a chosen script into a tape recorder, then find a comfortable chair in a quiet space where you will not be interrupted and play the tape back to yourself. You can also record a warmup and script and listen to it with your partner.

The visualizations that follow should each be done separately, one at a time. I recommend doing only one per day. After each guided visualization, I recommend you jot down your thoughts or feelings or record them orally, so before beginning have either a pad and pen or a recorder handy.

I recommend that you read the scripted material more slowly than you would read normally. Treat each period or comma as a distinct "pause" signal. Longer pauses—between thirty seconds and two minutes—are signified in this section with the sign ">".

Warmup

Sit comfortably in an upright position. If possible, loosen your clothing so that you are feeling as relaxed as possible. Feel free to close your eyes when you are ready to do so. You can open or close your eyes at any time if you wish. I recommend that you return to an eyes-closed position. You also can shift your body so that you find the most comfortable position for yourself and, if this changes and you feel that moving would make you more comfortable, by all means do so. Now breathe in through your nose and out through your mouth. Don't try to change or control your breath. Breathe in a natural rhythm. Simply pay attention to your breath. Nothing more, nothing less—attention to your breath. Nice, easy breaths. Notice your in-breath through the nose and your out-breath through the mouth. Notice that your stomach rises and falls as you breathe. That's good. Just keep your focus on your breath for a moment. If you feel any tension any-where in your body, simply be aware of it. If you'd like to shift, please do. If you'd prefer not to move, that's fine, too. Keep coming back to a focus on your breath. That's good. Now, I'd like you to imagine that as you breathe in, you are taking in more and more relaxation. You are breathing in a feeling of well-being. And as you breathe out, you can imagine that with the out-breath you are expelling any worries. You are able to release any worries. Nothing to do but pay attention to your breath. That's all there is to do. If your attention strays, that's okay. Let it come back. Don't force anything but allow your attention to return to your breathing. And to breathing in relaxation and breathing out anything that needs release. For right now, there is nothing to worry about and nothing to do but pay attention to your breath and allow the relaxation to come in and the worry to leave. Nothing else to do right now. And if you'd like, you can enjoy the feeling of letting go of tension, releasing tension. And you can enjoy the feeling of having the in-breath nurture you. That's good. . . . Keep that rhythm going. . . . I'm going to give you a minute to enjoy the rhythm of your breathing, and then we are going to do something else together. >

Guided Visualization #1

Envision the Greeting and More

Now that you are relaxed, take a moment to think of a memory or specific image that captures how you greet your partner. Within your mind, see yourself looking toward your partner as he approaches. Notice the expression on your face as your partner approaches. What is your greeting like? Do you imagine yourself feeling comfortable as your partner approaches you? Almost as if you were seeing the scene unfold in slow motion, give yourself all the time you need to read the expression on your face and think about what it means. Think about how you are feeling at this moment. >

As your partner approaches you, now focus your visual attention on your partner's face. It is as if you can see not only the expression but the thoughts and feelings that go with the expression. You somehow have full access to your partner's state of mind. Can you describe the way she feels as she approaches you? Can you imagine some of the thoughts that go along with those feelings? Are you imagining a meeting that is comfortable, a reunion of sorts? Are you imaging a meeting that feels uncomfortable? That is laced with sadness? Or anxiety? Or any other feeling? Even if there are difficult feelings, do you detect love in your partner? Do you detect love within yourself—even if it is not the only feeling that you experience—is there a trace or more of love within your mind-set at this moment? If there is such a feeling, appreciate it for a moment. Breathe with the loving feeling, even if it is a small feeling right now. If it is difficult to feel a loving feeling, ask yourself what the obstacle to feeling this love is. Ask yourself what the obstacle to allowing a loving feeling to be felt at this time might be. Now, in your mind's eye, allow the picture that you see to gradually disappear. Allow it to fade but remember what you have seen so that you can talk about it later if you would like to. Now go back to thinking about your breathing and breathing in relaxation and breathing out anything that is better released. >

Now think of the situation, the room or the doorway or the outdoor space; however you imagine it is okay. Imagine that you are having this meeting with your partner. And let your mind's eye wander around the place where you are. Is it a friendly, inviting place where you feel comfortable and welcome? Is it not a friendly and inviting place? Let your imagination direct you through the details of your surroundings. Let yourself see what is there for you and your partner. Have you chosen a good place to meet? Does the setting match the way you feel about you and your partner? If yes, think about how it matches. If not, think about a place that would be a better match. Think about a place that would help you both create the mood that you would like to create together. Now think about what that mood is. Let yourself think about what that mood is while you breathe comfortably in and out. That mood that you would like to experience with your partner, have you experienced that mood together? Think of the time or times when you shared the mood that you would like to create together. What would be needed to create such a mood with your partner, in your mind, at this time? Let yourself imagine a scene in which something very good happens, and you find yourself enjoying this time with your partner in a way that you have longed to do. Think about allowing these thoughts to float effortlessly around you. Allow yourself to imagine that things can begin to feel more and more like you would like them to feel. And as you think about that for a moment, and as you continue to breathe, I want to tell you that, in just a moment or two, I would like you to write down—or speak into a tape recorder—the thoughts and feelings that came up for you today as we went through our guided visualization. Continue to enjoy your relaxing breath for a moment, and whenever you are ready, open your eyes and take a count of ten before you jot down or record your thoughts and feelings. >

Guided Visualization #2

Note: This exercise, as written, describes an interaction between a man and a woman, but it can be easily customized to focus on a man-to-man or a woman-to-woman relationship. The exercise is used and described in detail in chapter 3.

The Pink Sun

After experiencing the warmup, begin this visualization.

Imagine you are holding a book. In your mind's eye, hold the book in front of you. You are holding the book in front of you, but it is as if the book is weightless. Holding it is effortless. Feel free to notice that, as you look at it, you can see the cover. Imagine it in a shade that you find very pleasing to you. In whatever color you imagine the cover to be, imagine a flower of that same hue and imagine its scent wafting up to you now. >

With eyes closed, imagine that the book is open before you. Now, lower the book onto a table that appears in front of you. Imagine that you are sitting in a comfortable chair and before you there is a table; on the table, the book is open, and you are looking at the pages before you. You see an illustration, in a mosaic design. It depicts a couple—a man and a woman. You are looking at an exquisite rendering of a couple who care very much about each other. In the illustration, you can see that their expressions are alive and seem to change from a still picture to a moving picture. You look at the picture, and you can see that there is so much about each other that the couple understands. And that there is so much about each other that they do not understand. And you are signaled by the picture that they are aware of this also. They themselves are coming to terms with the fact that they both know each other very well and, in another sense, have so much to learn about each other. >

We look at this picture and can see that the couple is having a hard time. The couple is having difficulties. Sometimes they feel angry. Sometimes disappointed. Each wonders whether they will be able to work things out. They wonder about how things will develop between them. And their thoughts float through the mosaic sky. There are many shades of blue in the sky. So many different lovely shades of color. Imagine the colors. Imagine their thoughts, even their worries, floating out into the sky there. Think about how they feel standing together under the beautiful sky. >

We turn the page and see the couple talking together. We see traces of steam floating out when they talk. It must be a cold day. When their words hit the air, steam rises up. The sky is no longer blue but silver grey. They cannot hear each other. All they know of each other's words is the sight of the steam rising. Words disappear into thin air. They face each other, unable to understand what is being said from one to the other, from the other back to the first. Again and again, their messages rise up and float away. And neither understands what the other is trying to get across. They both feel frustrated and then angry. They look up at the wisps of steam rising off and away as if maybe they'd be able to comprehend something of the words that they may represent. And then they are looking up and have lost sight of each other completely. They are staring out into silver grey sky. They push out greater and greater quantities of air, but these gestures billow up and float away just as readily as the smaller puffs of steam. This is what we see of the two as they try repeatedly to get across to each other. >

Tears of frustration form and drip down each of their faces. The wind blows cold. Imagine the wind nudging against them, causing them to take the gloves out of their pockets and put them on their hands. Imagine them pulling hats down over their ears. Finally, the wind comes up strong, and the two are pushed along. Let this image— the image of the two faltering as they walk into the distance—let this image settle in you a moment. >

We turn the page again and see that the couple has walked a great distance. They have come to an ocean or bay. The breezes are mild and gentle here. A sweet smell of fresh sea air comes wafting in toward them. They walk along together by the sea. The winter storm has given way to a balm of springtime. Imagine an oasis. Imagine a place in which all sense of desperation dissipates. Imagine feeling that just as strongly as the surroundings have seemed to make things difficult before, they now make things easier. The ordinary had been impossible. Now the extraordinary may be possible. >

We turn the page again and see a huge horizon beneath a lovely pink sun laid out across the water. Each wonders how they can make their relationship better. Each is having thoughts and feelings about how to do this. They stroll down near the foam. See them walk along the beach as clearly as possible. Imagine that you have a high-powered telescope and can now zoom in and read their faces. You intuit that what is happening between them makes each feel easier. And each breathes easier. They stand by the sea and gaze at the sunset. Far off at the side of the water, they can see traces of pink flicker against the outline of the moon. For a moment, the sky possesses a crescent of moon and a sliver of sun. The couple walks farther along the beach together. You can see them walk slowly down the coastline. The waves splash lightly on the beachhead. Each feels this moment as calm and peaceful. Notice the color of the sand. Study the image as if you were trying to memorize it within you. Take note of all the details of the scene. >

Turning the page again, we see the couple sitting in a room. They feel comfortable there and with one another. Imagine it a room that you might like to occupy. It can be a room that you are familiar with, a room you've been in before, or a room that you create using your imagination. Judging by their posture and their facial expressions, they have overcome something. Something that came into their life and caused problems for them has disappeared, faded from them in a way similar to how the steam that left their lips rose up and swirled out into the sky. There was something that they needed to get across to each other that they had great difficulty getting across to each other. Now that has been accomplished. Messages have gone back and forth and back again. Understandings have been established, and there is a feeling of having returned to each other. There is a feeling of relief that is palpable to both. Can you imagine that feeling that each of them is sharing? Take a deep breath and see if you can allow yourself to feel that a new feeling has entered into the way they feel together. >

It is a surprise for them to be experiencing this now. But it is a surprise that makes sense to both of them. It is a surprise that they each welcome. They do not have to make room to accommodate this new thing that has grown between them because it feels right. It is now the way it needs to be. It is now the way that they were hoping that it could be. Even though they may not have been able to explain exactly what that would mean. And they might not—even in this scene—be able to explain to anyone what they are feeling. It is a safe and easy feeling they share. They might say that. And that would be part of it. Safe and easy in each other's presence; yes, they are that. They each lean casually toward the other. Imagine them in the room. Are they sitting close to each other? Are they holding hands? Talking? Looking into each other's eyes? Laughing? Hugging? What are they thinking? There is no right or wrong way to imagine this scene. Give yourself to the freedom to imagine it any way you'd like. >

Take a moment to imagine how they helped themselves. I'm going to stop talking for a minute and give you a chance to imagine that. They are on the other side of an enormous challenge. Imagine how they feel in their bodies. Imagine that so much of their fear has melted. Focus on this for a moment. >

In a few moments, whenever you feel ready, I would like you to open your eyes. After you open your eyes, I would like you to jot down some of your thoughts, feelings, and impressions that you take with you from the visualization.

Guided Visualization #3

The New Light

Begin this visualization by using the warmup.

Imagine that you and your partner are sitting in a room together, and you are in the midst of an argument. Now imagine that there is background color to your argument. Let's say it is a scarlet light that is bathing the room behind you, the backdrop for your argument. Take a moment to imagine that red light behind you. It is forming the background for your conversation. Your argument feels harsh. A harsh shade of red, the color matches the tenor of the argument between you and your partner. It is almost like a mirror, in color, of the harsh tone of your argument and the raw state of your feelings in this argument. Imagine the color growing. You no longer can see you and your partner arguing but only the red light, which is a sort of visual equivalent for the conversation that had been going on. >

Visualize yourself and your partner again in the same room. Now the color behind you is crimson, close to the shade it had been, but a little bit softer. The tone is still within the red family, but the backdrop of light is much less harsh than it had been. Imagine that your conversation follows this change in color. The words had been harsh and sometimes loud. Now the conversation is getting softer. The harshness is leaving both the form and content of the sentences you say to each other. The words are unimportant; it is all in the tone that the meaning is conveyed here, and the tone matches the color that flows around you both. >

Now see something very interesting. See the colors become blends of color, swirls of color. As if it were a show of hand-blown and exotically colored glass sculptures swirling in the air, a swirling rainbow of color. The light has changed from harsh red to a mélange of beautiful streams of soothing color. Take a moment to see the swirl of color. >

Allow the swirl to calm into one shade that is particularly pleasing to you. A color that is a favorite of yours. A color that is soothing to you. Imagine sitting in the room you have seen earlier; where the light had been harsh and red, it now is soft and soothing. Where the conversation had been harsh and difficult, imagine now a conversation that would go well with this new light, this new mood. Take a moment to notice your breath and give your attention to the mood that goes with this new light. After you do this, imagine the *feeling* of a conversation that would follow in this light. The words are not important right now; imagine the mood and the flow. Imagine a stillness that is filled with this color if you can. >

Hold onto that new light for a moment and then let it go. Allow an image of harshness to come. Then allow it to transform into softness. This is symbolic of what your communication can be like in the middle ground with you and your partner focusing on connecting rather than winning or losing a struggle. With you and your partner focusing on connecting, rather than proving or disproving who is right or wrong. If you should argue, remember that you can shift your focus, if the conversation is not a productive one, from the words to the emotional color tone, and that will often give the conversation a new life and make it work for you. Allow the colors that are within your communication to inform you about what you need to do in order to connect. >

Feel free to open your eyes whenever you feel ready to do so. After you open your eyes, take a pen and paper—or your tape recorder—and make note of the feelings you had while on this guided visualization. Think about how you can use this exercise when you are together, with your partner, and you should have an argument. You will have a new tool to work with that can make things better for you.

Guided Visualization #4

The New Sound

Begin the visualization by using the warmup.

Imagine that you and your partner are sitting in a room, and you are in the midst of an argument. Now imagine that there is a background sound that—in tone and texture—closely matches the emotional tone of what you are saying to each other. The sound is caustic and irritating. In much the same way that the argument feels irritating and discomforting. Imagine a sound that you particularly dislike— chalk on a blackboard or perhaps a stringed instrument like a violin played out of tune so that it sounds like prolonged scratching. Perhaps even the sound of a person in discomfort. Once you have been able to imagine a sound like this—an unpleasant sound—take a moment to stay with it. Imagine that sound starting out as a small but definite presence. Now imagine it as growing in intensity until it fills up the space. Now imagine it receding into the background. >

Now tune into your breathing and allow yourself to settle into visualizing sitting with your partner once more in the same room. Only this time the sound in the room has changed from what it had been into something softer. The tone is in some way related to the previous discomforting sound, but now it is becoming less harsh, less grating. Also imagine that the conversation with your partner, which had been angry, is now toning down. The conversation is becoming softer; it is expressive but not adversarial. The words are unimportant, but the tone of the words and the timbre of voice is warmer. As the conversation flows around the room, you sense that the sound in the room is becoming distinctly more pleasing, more musical. >

Now take a moment to imagine that the pleasant element of the new sound is changing even further into a tone that is soothing and evocative. And other sound qualities can be perceived as joining the first in a harmony or structure of some kind that is pleasing. The musical sounds fill the room with what feels like an invitation to breathe deeply and relax with the sounds. Whatever types or textures of sound you find enjoyable, please imagine that they are filling the room at this time. Simply enjoy the swirl of sounds. Like a collage of sounds that you enjoy. >

Imagine sitting in the room as you had earlier with your partner and, with the pleasing sounds in the background, imagine—without trying to hear the words—that the conversation you are having with your partner is synchronized, emotionally, with the sounds flowing around. The words that you say to each other encourage each of you to listen and take in the other's message. There is no tension in the room, and the message that you wish to get across seems to flow easily, just as the music of the room flows. Imagine that the music is as lively or as calming as you wish it to be. Imagine that—if you would like it to be so—it is as soft and soothing as the sound of a gentle sea, or of water flowing gently in a country brook. If you wish, imagine a room of silence, where the entire dimension of sound is gentle and even beautiful in its absence, if this makes sense to you. Enjoy whatever sounds you imagine or the stillness that surrounds you if you prefer. >

Recall the sound image of harshness that you had experienced earlier. Now imagine it shifting into the softer sound and then to the pleasing sound. The soothing elements, the enlivening communicative elements of sound can be like what communication in the middle ground can bring to you and your partner as you focus on connecting rather than winning or losing an argument. With you and your partner focusing on connecting, rather than proving or disproving who is right or wrong. Now, if you should argue, remember that you can shift your focus. If the conversation feels unfriendly or unproductive, give yourself an opportunity to associate the words that are being spoken with the emotional tenor—the sound ambience—that would match the conversation. Focus on that ambient sound quality and think about what it would take to shift from the harshness or coldness into something that would be more soothing, more productive. Think of how the sounds would have to shift in order to put the conversation on a more productive footing and try to match that new direction with the words you utter. Or simply call attention to this underlying element in the conversation and ask your partner to help change the tone of where the conversation is or where it seems to be headed. >

Feel free to open your eyes whenever you feel ready to do so. After you open your eyes, take a pen and paper—or your tape recorder—and make note of the feelings you had while on this guided visualization. Think about how you can use this exercise when you are together with your partner and you have an argument. You will have a new tool to work with that can make things better for you.

Appendix 3

YOUR RELATIONAL AUTOIMMUNE SYSTEM

For many couples, everyday problems expose the absence of any mechanism in the communication process for safely airing or resolving grievances. With no safe space in your relationship to examine differences, terrors of abandonment arise. In this atmosphere, fear grows unchecked. Emotional safety departs entirely, even from memory. Bitterness finds a central place in ordinary discourse. Remnants of goodwill corrode. Minor difficulties run deeper than warranted or reasonable. By contrast, within the middle ground, couples learn to differentiate between major and minor impasses and respond accordingly.

IN THE MIDDLE OF MINOR DIFFERENCES

The middle ground opens pathways to reconnect after a couple experiences ordinary misunderstandings, lapses in contact, genuine differences of perspective.

According to Amanda, "I can't be in the car with the window closed. I need the air. I realize that Carl prefers the window closed, but I don't feel like it means as much to him."

Amanda sounds reasonable. When I ask her how she knows that Carl doesn't care as much as she does, she doesn't have an answer. When I ask Carl about it, he says that it is important to him, that he feels uncomfortable with the wind blowing on his face and eyes. "And," he adds, "Amanda has ideas about what I'm feeling and shows no interest in finding out whether what she's thinking matches what I actually feel. It's as if who I really am doesn't matter. That gets me angry."

"Would it make a difference," I wonder out loud, "if Amanda were to ask you about how you felt about the window?"

Carl replies, "Probably."

Then I asked Amanda, "Do you feel that Carl understands what you feel when you ask him to leave the window open?"

Amanda says, "He doesn't know because he's never asked. He doesn't seem to care enough to ask."

"You both seem to feel hurt that your partner has taken very little initiative in finding out what your personal experience of this situation has been," I say. "It seems both of you feel unappreciated and almost like you're with a stranger who has no knowledge or interest in what is really going on inside of you."

Both Amanda and Carl nod in agreement.

"I have a feeling that what bothers you both more than whether the window is open or closed is that neither of you is reaching out to make contact with the other, and you both feel alone and uncared for when these arguments happen."

Amanda and Carl turn toward each other. A flash of reciprocal communication occurs.

Opening a middle-ground area exposes the emotional basis of a disagreement; opportunities for mutual understanding arise, and small disagreements and misunderstandings can be kept in perspective. The middle ground serves Carl and Amanda—and all couples—as a relational autoimmune system. If a couple sustains (or develops) faith in their ability to pick themselves up and resume their journey together after minor setbacks, confidence in their identity as a couple grows.

The middle ground strengthens a couple's sense of identity and purpose—one experience at a time, one connection at a time.

In the face of trying situations—losses, differences in parenting styles, money problems, infidelity—partners feel less vulnerable to feelings of hopelessness, less alone with their problems if a middle ground has already been established. Coping with the ordinary generates stamina needed for grappling with the extraordinary. Coping depends, much of the time, on communication.

Note: Each of the communication exercises in this book offers a means for helping you to locate, strengthen, and maintain your relational autoimmune system.

Appendix 4

WHAT TO DO IF YOUR PARTNER IS ABUSIVE

If you are reading this section and identify with being in an abusive relationship, ask yourself this: Am I responding to my situation as if it were a crisis? If the answer is no, then ask yourself why not. And do something about it. (Reread the section on codependency.) If you are not responding to your situation as if it were a crisis, then you may well be enabling the abuse to continue.

If you are in doubt about whether your relationship should be considered abusive or not, I urge you to contact a licensed therapist in your area or to write me at my website (www.powerofthemiddle ground.com), and I will try to help you figure this out.

Response to abuse requires action. Behavioral changes are necessary. After you've secured your safety, it may be possible to think about middle-ground potential for the future, depending on how damaging the relationship is and other factors. But nothing can be attempted unless safety is secured. If you need help immediately, call 911. Other sources of help:

National Domestic Violence Hot Line: 1-800-799-7233
Support Network for Battered Women: 1-800-572-2782
Drug and Alcohol Resource Center: 1-800-784-6776

Appendix 5

SELECT RECOMMENDED READINGS

This list is highly subjective and personal. I will update it periodically on my Web site, http://www.powerofthemiddleground.com.

Beattie, Melody. *Codependent No More*. New York: MJF Books, 1997. I believe that Melody Beattie coined the term *codependency*. Personal and moving accounts of dealing with issues relating to addiction and codependency.

Dym, Barry, and Michael L. Glenn. *Couples: Exploring and Understanding the Cycles of Intimate Relationships*. New York: HarperCollins, 1993. A sleeper. Excellent discussion of marital dynamics.

Gottman, John. *Seven Principles for Making Marriage Work*. New York: Three Rivers Press, 1999. Gottman is a prolific researcher and writer. Everything that he writes is worthwhile. His books are extremely user friendly. Many valuable concepts and interesting research results.

Jacobs, John W. *All You Need Is Love and Other Lies about Marriage*. New York: HarperCollins, 2004. Along with Terrance Real's book (below), this is the most contemporary general discussion that includes social perspective and historical development of the institution of marriage. Highly recommended.

Lerner, Harriet, *The Dance of Anger.* New York: HarperCollins, 1985. The first in her series of excellent books on relationship dynamics; all are valuable.

Love, Patricia, and Jo Robinson. *Hot Monogamy.* New York: Plume, 1994. Extremely well organized and coherent. Friendly tone along with incisive insights into relationship dynamics. A classic.

Real, Terrence. *The New Rules of Marriage: What You Need to Know to Make Love Work.* New York: Ballantine, 2007. A tough-minded but also tender-hearted approach to contemporary relationship problems. A top choice.

Schnarch, David. *The Passionate Marriage.* New York: Norton, 1997. Important theoretical and practical discussions help readers untangle feelings and thoughts related to relational problems from feelings related to family-of-origin issues.

Schwartz, Barry. *The Paradox of Choice: Why More Is Less.* New York: HarperCollins, 2004. An excellent discussion of how we Americans make our decisions—from the way we choose to pursue our purchases to the way we choose to pursue our relationships. Well written and insightful.

Stone, Douglas, et al. *Difficult Conversations: How to Discuss What Matters Most.* New York: Penguin Books, 2000. This book lays out great strategies for understanding and learning how to engage productively in conversation and negotiation in public and private situations. A model of clear and clever organization and presentation. I can't recommend it highly enough.

Tannen, Deborah. *You Just Don't Understand,* New York: HarperCollins, 1990. This book explains much about differences in the ways that men and women communicate.

Wachtel, Ellen. *We Love Each Other, But—*. New York: St. Martin's, 1999. Down-to-earth, smart, and upbeat.

Wallerstein, Judith, and Sandra Blakeslee. *The Good Marriage: How and Why Love Lasts*. New York: Warner Books, 1996. A good overview of the authors' account of the elements that go into making a marriage succeed.

Wile, Daniel. *After the Fight: A Night in the Life of a Couple*. New York: Guildford, 1993. A clear thinker; not an ounce of pretension; much intelligence and compassion; helpful, low-key. The entire book is dedicated to analyzing a marital fight. The author lays out his approach, as well as how he strives to help each partner develop and articulate their point of view and join one another in preserving their love.

INDEX